The Power of Your Money Game

Use Gamification & Game Thinking to Gain Wealth & Elevate Your Influence … Escape the Money Rat Race & Reach Your Income Goals

Use the "Gamify Your Wealth System"

from GetTheBigYES.com

Tom Marcoux
Communication Sage – Spoken Word Strategist
International Speaker – Author of 50+ books
Novelist – Screenwriter – Feature Film Director

A QuickBreakthrough Publishing Edition

ISBN-13: 978-0-9624660-8-3

QuickBreakthrough Publishing is an imprint of Tom Marcoux Media, LLC. More copies are available from the publisher, Tom Marcoux Media, LLC. Please write to TomSuperCoach@gmail.com
or visit Tom's blogs: GettheBigYES.com
www.YourBodySoulandProsperity.com PitchPowerFest.com
This book was developed and written with care. Names and details were modified to respect privacy.

Other Books by Tom Marcoux:
• Darkest Secrets of Film Directing
• Darkest Secrets of Making a Pitch to the Film / TV Industry
• What the Rich Don't Say about Getting Rich
• Relax, You Don't Need to Sell (Make Sales without Being Pushy) … with Authentic Marketing
• Shape the Future, Lead Like a Pro (with Authentic Leadership)
• Darkest Secrets of Persuasion and Seduction Masters

From The Tom Marcoux Institute (online courses):

- Success Secrets: Confidence and Skills to Handle Toxic People
- Ignite Your Sales Success
- Convince Investors to Fund You
- Darkest Secrets of Persuasion and Seduction Masters: How to Protect Yourself and Turn the Power to Good

Go to **GetTheBigYES.com/courses**

Praise for *The Power of Your Money Game*

• "*The Power of Your Money Game* reveals secrets so powerful you can free yourself from the poverty thinking that holds you back. Marcoux gives you the tools to elevate your influence. The best part is Marcoux makes techniques so practical and easy to remember. This is life changing."
– Jonathan Colton, entrepreneur and author

• "Tom Marcoux's book is enlightening. You learn to overcome procrastination. He helps you get in the game. Get this book!."
– David Chametzky, TEDx Speaker, Deep Message Coach, author of *When Your Heart Says "It's Your Time to Soar!"*

Praise for Tom Marcoux's Other Books:

• "In *Darkest Secrets of Persuasion and Seduction Masters: How to Protect Yourself and Turn the Power to Good*, learn how to defend yourself against manipulation." – Dr. JoAnn Dahlkoetter, Coach to CEOs and Olympic Gold Medalists

• "In *Connect*, Tom's advice on how to remain true to yourself and establish authentic rapport with clients is both insightful and reality based. He [shows how] to establish oneself as a credible expert."
– Arthur P. Ciaramicoli, Ed.D., Ph.D., author *The Stress Solution*

• "Concerned about networking situations? Get *Relax Your Way Networking.* Success is built on high trust relationships. Master Coach Tom Marcoux reveals secrets to increase your influence."
– Greg S. Reid, Author, *Think and Grow Rich Series*

• "In *Reduce Clutter, Enlarge Your Life*, Marcoux will help you get rid of the physical and mental clutter occupying precious space in your life. You'll reclaim wasted energy, lower your stress, and find time for new opportunities." – Laura Stack, author of *Execution IS the Strategy*

• "Tom Marcoux is a master at systems. His book, *The Writer's Solution: Crush Your Self-Doubt* is a step-by-step plan of how to quiet down the fears… He offers tangible solutions in helping the reader to just get the book down on paper… His authentic approach has been both encouraging and supportive. I highly recommend this book." – Joie Gharrity, author

From The Tom Marcoux Institute (online courses):

- Success Secrets: Confidence and Skills to Handle Toxic People
- Ignite Your Sales Success
- Convince Investors to Fund You
- Darkest Secrets of Persuasion and Seduction Masters: How to Protect Yourself and Turn the Power to Good

Go to GetTheBigYES.com/courses

Visit Tom's blogs: **GetTheBigYES.com** **PitchPowerFest.com**

DEDICATION AND ACKNOWLEDGMENTS

This work is dedicated to YOU. Here are Special Offers:

- Get your FREE Gift – Access the VIDEO "Protect Yourself from Poisoners of Your Wealth" Go to: http://GetTheBigYES.com/protect_yourself
- Apply for a **Free Hidden Breakthrough Strategy Session** with Tom Marcoux https://GetTheBigYES.com/nextstep

This book is also dedicated to the terrific Video/Audio Strategist and author Johanna E. Mac Leod. Thanks to Johanna E. Mac Leod for this book's cover and for guidance. Thanks to the notable people who were interviewed. Thanks to Jonathan Colton, David Chametzky, David Barron, Benson Wong, Kevin Trivedi, Bob Choat, Dave Thude, and Mike Lamothe for your support and guidance. Thanks to my parents. Thank you to Higher Power … and to our readers, audiences, clients, my graduate students, and my team members of The Tom Marcoux Institute and GetTheBigYES.com. Many great moments to you.

The methods and insights in this book are emphasized in online courses at The Tom Marcoux Institute.

Go to **GetTheBigYES.com/courses**

The Power of Your Money Game (Secrets of Gamify Your Wealth)

What if you could remove obstacles to your creating wealth? Creating wealth is one minute at a time.

A minute is precious.

For example, some years ago, I experienced this:

"Michael is going to die."

Oblivious, Michael stood behind the viewfinder of his camera as an airplane wing came screaming toward his head. I was the first-time feature film director.

The small plane wing was supposed to go over the feature film camera and his head. But standing tall, he was about to be hit.

If I yelled, he might turn my way and get hit by the wing. So, I dropped my binder, ran, and grabbed his jacket. I pulled down, and the wing cut the air where our heads had just been.

This was one of the most important moments of my life.

This moment now is vital to you. How? This book is designed to help you create real wealth—from moment to

moment. I shared the airplane experience because it demonstrates *essential elements of creating wealth.*

- Do the right thing.
- No hesitation to go into action.
- Stop being distracted.

To create wealth, you must consistently take action.

Can you find yourself saying these ideas?

I want financial abundance. I want hope. I want measurable progress.

Imagine you could drop the shackles of doubt and past failures or inaction.

In this book, I will introduce you to the *power* that will help you consistently take effective action. Then, you will be trustworthy to yourself. This also leads others to trust you. Then, they want to see you succeed. You'll gain real support.

What is this power?

It's the ***Power of Gamification.***

Plus, you'll learn to use the **Power to Elevate Your Influence.**

I was able to direct my first feature film on that runway because I developed:

- Skills to create rapport and radiate confidence so people would support me in making the film
- Skills to communicate my trustworthiness
- Reliable methods so I did tough stuff—write the script, revise it, and do all the "chores" required to get things done
- Learning from effective people who achieved what I wanted to achieve

This book puts you into the "director's chair" of your

blossoming life of financial abundance.

To support your learning essential methods, I have interviewed effective people. This book includes guidance from a billionaire and millionaires I have personally learned from. I interviewed them. I asked them questions. The answers are here in this book.

This book gives you a unique advantage. You'll learn to employ the elements of gamification, so you do effective actions to create true wealth.

"Games are the most elevated form of investigation."
– Albert Einstein

Soon, I will provide definitions of wealth and gamification.

Before that, let's see how this material works.

My thousands of clients, students, and workshop attendees get real and powerful results.

These Methods Gain Results:

- "I'm truly grateful to Tom Marcoux for essential tips that helped me win the Grand Prize of the Pitch Competition—the Igniter Summit in Bangkok, Thailand." – Neeraj Aggarwala, CEO/Founder of Sportido
- "Tom Marcoux has coached me to make my speeches compelling and powerful. He has helped me prepare for the media. Do your career a big favor and engage Tom Marcoux, the Spoken Word Strategist." – Dr. JoAnn Dahlkoetter, Sports Psychologist, author of *Your Performing Edge* and Coach to CEOs and Olympic Gold Medalists

Let's begin.

Chapter 1

Get Started with the W.E.A.L.T.H. System – Work with Your New-Found Confidence

At 9 years old, I trembled sitting at the piano. At a retirement facility, thirty-one senior citizens stared at me.

I was terrified. My leg fluttered so fast, like a hummingbird's wings.

I played the piano, and my right foot was on the sustain pedal. At any moment, it would slip off and cause a THUD sound.

Then, they would think I was an idiot and a moron.

The idiot couldn't play the notes right.

And the moron couldn't keep his foot on the sustain pedal!

So, I started shy, timid—and displaying introverted tendencies.

So, of course, I would become a speaker, lecturer to MBA students (Stanford University and other universities), and a leading actor. Oh, a feature film director, too.

I had to train with mentors.

Years ago, I remember when multi-millionaire Guy Kawasaki told me, "I'm one of the only people to work for Steve Jobs twice and survive."

He went on to emphasize: "Know your customers well enough to satisfy the needs they cannot even express. Then get to know your customers again to satisfy the changes and upgrades they can express."

I took notes.

Additionally, Guy Kawasaki is known for originating the 10/20/30 Rule for sales and pitching.

The 10/20/30 rule of PowerPoint is: "No PowerPoint presentation should be more than ten slides, longer than 20 minutes, and use fonts smaller than 30-point size."

I got two things from this Rule. First, the content about what works in marketing. Second, when you communicate something make it short and memorable ("10/20/30 Rule").

New in the film industry, I received coaching from George Takei, Mr. Sulu of ***Star Trek***, the original series. What did that coaching do? It helped me complete my first feature film. It also helped me save money and not waste resources on the set. (I'll tell you more about that later.)

At Stanford University, while teaching MBA students, I used methods that would become **part of the essence of my science Code Access Reset™. I have developed this science and gained proven results.**

For example, one of my students gained a position at Donna Karan International in New York City. She used the methods I taught her at the Academy of Art University. These techniques helped her turn her job interviewer into a coach for the next rounds of interviews.

Let's jump in, and learn and excel with *confidence.*

In Thailand, speaking at the Corporate Innovation Summit, I said,

Confidence is not comfort.
Confidence is a toolkit.
And you work it.

To be confident with people and grow your wealth, you can use my C.A.N. System

C – curiosity
A – advantage
N – nurture relationship

Example of the C.A.N. System:

I wanted to develop a relationship with a Hollywood Screenwriter. I sent him a text:

I have a new idea that helps fellow writers and

All three elements of C.A.N. are used here:

a) A new idea (Curiosity)
b) Ending the text with "and" (Curiosity)
c) "a new idea that helps fellow writers" (Advantage)
d) "fellow writers" (Nurture relationship…I am a fellow writer—we have a connection as writers.)

Did this text work?
Yes. He replied with a simple "?"
I called him.
We have developed a friendship, I'm glad to say.

1. Curiosity

You need a "hook" to get the person's attention. Make them curious. How is this going to turn out? What value can I get from this?

2. Advantage

Survive. That is the call of our brain and our body. Show the person that there is a personal advantage for them. It's worth talking with you for their true benefit.

3. Nurture relationship

Even a one-minute conversation is a "relationship."

"I've learned that people will forget what you said, people will forget what you did, but people will never forget how you made them feel." – Maya Angelou

How do you nurture a relationship? Make the person feel that you care—and that they are important to you.

Now, you've heard about the C.A.N. System... What will you do with the knowledge?

At Hacker Dojo in Silicon Valley, California, I said,

Knowledge is just noise unless you can recall it instantly.

This is where gamification comes in.

When you use gamification, you can ensure that you do an effective action.

What is an effective action? In this case, you make sure to memorize a vital, helpful Trio of Principles.... C.A.N. – Curiosity, Advantage, Nurture Relationship.

Let's look at ...

The Definition of Gamification:

"The application of typical elements of game playing (e.g. point scoring, competition with others, rules of play) to

other areas of activity, typically as an online marketing technique to encourage engagement with a product or service.

'gamification is exciting because it promises to make the hard stuff in life fun'" – Oxford Languages

When I say, "Gamify Your Wealth," I'm talking about using gamification to ensure that you accomplish effective actions. You can increase your current level of financial abundance.

Wealth also means more than one's financial status.

The Definition of Wealth:
"An abundance of valuable possessions or money.
...the state of being rich; material prosperity.
...plentiful supplies of a particular resource."
– Oxford Languages

In this section, let's realize that to gain wealth in terms of money (for example), it's important to have a *wealth of skills*. What type of skills? **Skills to Elevate Your Influence.**

Many wealthy people are excellent communicators. That's how they get what they want. They can effectively lead people to get the vital things done.

The other side of excellent communication is to ***Communicate with Yourself on an Excellent Level.***

So, let's use gamification to make sure you *own* the ideas of C.A.N.

How does this look?

Gamify Grid #1 (Example)	
Action	Study the C.A.N. System once a day for three days.
Token	Use a quarter (coin). Place one quarter in jar per day after accomplishing your daily study of 5 minutes.
Date Start	11/21/20__
Date Completion	11/23/20__ (three days)
Self-Reward	Purchase 3 songs on iTunes

Now, let's dive deeper into this process.

To use gamification to do an action that makes you more skillful, you need 3 Elements. We S.E.T. the scene.

S – score
E – earn rewards
T – token

1. Score.

You can't win if you don't know the score. Wealthy people often say, "The money is how I keep score." At one point, I had an online class with one online retailer. I gained $4.00 per student. Then, I began hosting my courses myself. The return went from $4.00 to $800.00 per student. Yes, I knew the score. And my sweetheart really preferred knowing that our work was earning $800.00!

2. Earn rewards.

Many video game players experience real pleasure in seeing their scores rise. Dr. Anna Lembke, medical director of Stanford Addiction Medicine, emphasizes that "addiction is the continued and compulsive consumption of a substance or behavior." Why does this occur? She writes about the release of the neurotransmitter dopamine, which is part of the reward pathway in a person's brain.

Is watching your score rise addictive?

Many people experience a good feeling as a reward in that moment—when viewing one's score rise.

Why do you buy a shirt, a car, a home? Because of the feelings you anticipate you'll gain. Earning rewards is an essential part of playing the game.

Games researcher Robert Bartle noted four player types: achievers, explorers, socializers, and killers. **This has a real effect on what kind of "self-rewards" you give to yourself—to motivate your actions.**

"Achievers love the rush of leveling up or earning a badge; explores want to find new content; socializers want to engage with friends; and killers want to impose their will on others, typically by vanquishing them." – Kevin Werbach and Dan Hunter

What motivates you? What self-rewards would energize you?

3. Token

In my above example, the token was a quarter (coin). You can choose whatever token works well for you. A token is helpful—especially in sales. For example, you can have twenty coins and move them into your "Cold Calls for the day" jar…as you work during your work shift.

How does all this use of patterns improve your level of confidence?

Recently as I delivered my interactive workshop, *Convince Investors to Fund You,* I said,

Confidence is built on evidence. Prepare and *you know* you have an advantage.

So, the use of patterns is for your *preparation.*
The most prepared person wins.
And…
Courage is easier when you're prepared.

We're talking about *Elevate Your Influence.*

That means, we're talking about doing the actions necessary, so you communicate better. In that way, you can Elevate Your Influence.

* * * * * *

We'll now begin with Principle #1…

Gamify Your Wealth
Principle #1
Set the Score and Meaning

It's important to set a meaningful score. One can make the mistake of choosing the wrong target. It causes trouble to run enthusiastically in the wrong direction. Let's say you want to increase your business growth. You could set a score of posting twenty times a week at X (formerly Twitter), but this means nothing if your account focuses on the wrong audience.

So, the better plan is: Think it through and find a score

that can propel you forward effectively.

For example, one can set the score of *rehearse for 9 minutes a day* for the next fifteen days. You can become more specific: *Rehearse for 9 minutes a day in front of one of three people who offer good coaching.* Perhaps, you use Zoom for video conferencing.

Specifics help you set a meaningful score. They empower you to make real progress.

* * * * * *

Gamify Grid #2 (Example)	
Action	Read one chapter of The Power of Your Money Game each day
Token	Use a quarter (coin). Place one quarter in jar per day after accomplishing the daily reading
Date Start	11/22/20
Date Completion	11/26/20 (five days)
Self-Reward	Purchase 3 songs on iTunes

Now, it's your turn to fill out the Gamify Grid…

Gamify Grid	
Action	
Token	
Date Start	
Date Completion	
Self-Reward	

Important Points to Remember:

Confidence is built on evidence. Prepare and *you know*

you have an advantage.

Power Question:

How are you going to use the Gamify Grid to keep score and consistently do a vital action?

A side note: I write for business owners and others who like concise, memorable information. I do include a partial list of references at the end of this book.

Chapter 2

Use the W.E.A.L.T.H. System Work Your Confidence

"What do you do if your boss never listens to you—or anybody?" asked an attendee of my workshop for the Silicon Valley Chapter of the Project Management Institute.

My blood ran cold. I did not have an answer.

It's hard to be confident when you fumble in a speech—and you have no idea how to recover.

I was stuck.

I could have frozen like a deer in a car's headlights.

Instead, I said, "I need to pause for a moment. I want my response to be valuable to you."

I did *not* appear stuck.

By the time I finished saying those two sentences, I had the answer.

I said, "Quote your boss back to him. You can say, 'George, you know how you said ABC?'

He replies, 'Yeah.'

Then, you say, 'If we add 1-2-3 to it, it will go better.'
Then, your boss says, "Yeah. Do it.'"

I shared my above experience with you to demonstrate a point. You do *not* have to feel confident to act in a manner that "radiates confidence."

What you need is an Effective Method to Handle a Situation.

Transform Your Doubts and Fears from Past Situations about Growing Wealth

You have likely made some significant mistakes. Perhaps, you bought something—a car, a laptop computer---and it was a piece of junk.

You may have real fears about starting a business or going into a new field. Or getting a new job.

You can transform your doubts and fears when you have effective methods.

So, I'll ask you: Do you feel real doubt whether you can shake off the mistakes of the past and make real progress to develop real wealth?

If you do have some doubts, this book can help you. How?

This book helps you look up and "see a new horizon."

How does that work?

Picture this. You pick some actions that you discover in this book. You make progress. It's like you walk up the side of a mountain. When you rise out of the valley, you can see new peaks (new choices) that you could not see before. Why? You're no longer stuck in the valley.

You learn to take new actions. You make a shift in your mind.

At one point, I realized that I could make a shift in my mind by having positive answers to the following 4 Questions.

The 4 Wealth-Growing Questions:

1) Are you developing assets and relationships every week?
2) Are you creating "the Skillful You" each day?
3) Have you transformed your bad habits?
4) Are you doing better this month than last month?

To make this memorable, I say,

Be the person who A.C.T.S. in ways to grow wealth.

A.C.T.S.

A – assets and relationships
C – Create "the Skillful You"
T – transform bad habits
S – set "this month better than last month"

In the next chapters, we're going to dive deeper into Work Your Confidence.

By the way….

The W.E.A.L.T.H. System begins with

W – work your confidence

E – elevate your influence

I'll cover more as we go along.

Congratulations on your progress. Here is

Your Free Reward → See this Free Video:

Stay Strong and Confident: Strategies to Overcome the Lies by Tom Marcoux

Go to: http://GetTheBigYES.com/stay_strong

This video is from

Chapter 3

Use the W.E.A.L.T.H. System Work Your Confidence

(Assets and Relationships)

We begin with the "A" of A.C.T.S.

Assets and Relationships

Richard Carlson, the late author of *Don't Sweat the Small Stuff,* pulled me aside just before a radio show. We were both guest experts on this broadcast.

He had a best-selling series of books and more. Richard emphasized that it was important to build a foundation when you're a new speaker-author.

"Tom, you could find a small newspaper and be their expert columnist," Richard said. (This was some time ago.)

To this day, I remember two principles inspired by his guidance that he gave to me.

1) Form an alliance.

2) Be seen as a helpful expert.

In-person, Richard was just as you would hope a stress management expert would be. He was calm and friendly.

I talked with him a couple of times. I remember the first time I met him. He told the story of how he came up with the title of *Don't Sweat the Small Stuff.*

He mentioned how he asked best-selling author Dr. Wayne Dyer to give him a cover endorsement for one of his books.

Then, a short time later, to Richard's horror, the publisher put Wayne's endorsement on the wrong book.

Frantic, Richard called up Wayne. "Wayne, the publisher put your endorsement on the wrong book!"

"Don't sweat the small stuff," Wayne replied.

How about that? Wayne knew that Richard wrote good books. Wayne took a calm approach to the situation. A lesson for Richard. And a lesson for me, too.

Here's one of my favorite ideas Richard shared: "You are what you practice most."

I'm inviting you to practice essential actions to support your relationships.

In Silicon Valley, California (plus Thailand), I have delivered my interactive workshop *Convince Investors to Fund You* several times. I have also served as a Pitch Judge. That means I help founders of startup companies, as they prepare to pitch to investors, including venture capitalists.

Over and over, I pause when I hear the newbies make a certain mistake.

Without having a conversation, a newbie will blurt, "Hey, do you know anyone who wants to invest in a company?"

There is no conversation. No trust has been built. And no respect is shown.

The person who has contacts in the industry thinks: "Who are you? I don't know you. You want me to waste my personal contacts and the trust I built on a stranger?"

On the other hand, you can learn effective actions to build good relationships.

When I am addressing MBA students (for example, at Stanford University) or an industry gathering, I look to create a rapport.

Recently, during my interactive workshop *Ignite Your Sales Success: Avoid BIG Mistakes that Cost You Sales,* I talked about creating good relationships.

Once I had rapport with the audience, I said,

I'm the Communication Sage.
'Cause I lean into my age.
Don't come to me for theories.
I got wisdom for your queries.

The audience applauded. I broke into a big smile.

Life is so much about creating good relationships.

So how can you develop a good relationship? Listen.

Here is the C.A.R.E. process for listening:

C – continue to listen
A – ask follow-up questions
R – restrain from jumping in with an opinion
E – engage with "That sounds like…"

1. Continue to listen.

Avoid interrupting the person. You can ask, "Oh, is there anything else you'd like me to know?" Pause. Wait to see if the person is finished talking.

2. Ask follow-up questions.

How does the person know that you heard them? In part, they know when you ask a relevant follow-up question. It sounds like: "So when the vet said that your dog Emmy needed surgery how did that go?"

3. Restrain from jumping in with an opinion.

I often say,

I like to hold to perceptions. Give me new data, and I can easily change a perception. On the other hand, I know people who would sweat blood before changing an opinion.

It can be easy to jump in and tell a friend, "You know what? You should tell your boss to jump in the lake. He can't…"

It can be more important for you to listen. And your friend can find her own solutions. Or at least, she knows you care about her. You're supporting her. How? You're listening.

Here are my thoughts:

Listen first.

When you're listening, you're winning.

4. Engage with "That sounds like…"

We want to be heard. Respected. And supported. You can say something like: "That sounds like it was frustrating."

Then the person feels like their feelings were heard and that they matter.

We say, "That sounds like" because we are *not* telling that other person how they feel.

Sometimes, the person elaborates with "Not frustrating. It felt like a put-down."

Show you are listening—not just to the content of the message. You're listening to the feelings.

How to Engage a Top Industry Person

Years ago, as a producer, director, and writer, I was working on a feature film. One actor surprised me. She sent me information about a workshop on distribution and distributors. This was information I could use—as a producer and director.

She was looking out for my interests.

Later, I cast her in two productions. Why? Because she demonstrated a trustworthy quality. She also had skills and talent for acting. When you want to start a relationship with a highly effective person in an industry, pause. **Think of how you can help and enhance what *they* find important.** I have learned directly from many top individuals. How? I invited them to be a guest on my ***Succeed Even If*** **Podcast** and to have guest articles in my books. I serve *their priority* to promote their own work.

About Developing Your Relationships

When I interviewed billionaire Andres Pira, he emphasized: "I believe that if you want success, make other people successful. If it's money you want, help other people make money. If you want love, make sure to love yourself. Whatever you give comes back to you tenfold."

For more context …

Interview with Andres Pira, billionaire

Tom: What does it take to rise to high levels of achievement?

Andres Pira: I like setting 101 goals. Most people have to understand that you have to put small goals into any goal setting because when you only have bigger goals, they become very hard to obtain. Blend small goals with big goals. Because as soon as you complete small goals, it feels like you're moving forward, and then you can go to the bigger goal. You have the sense of moving forward every time. It gives you more confidence to achieve the bigger goals.

In my book, *Homeless to Billionaire,* I write about full-color goal setting. Many people set unspecific goals like gain a million dollars. It's very hard to get something if it is not clear in your mind. If you want a new car, what color is it? How does it look inside? How does it smell? How often will you drive it? How will it feel? So, you need to be specific with any goal setting. And that's how it will come much quicker to you.

Tom: What is an essential practice for creating success?

Andres: I believe that if you want success, make other people successful. If it's money you want, help other people make money. If you want love, make sure to love yourself. Whatever you give comes back to you tenfold.

Tom: What's next for you?

Andres: I consider myself a global citizen. Although I've built my empire in Southeast Asia, I don't see any possibilities within this world that are out of reach. The mindset is the most important gift I can contribute positively to both local and global society. A progressive shifting mindset from one person can make a wave. This is the moment. Now is the time I would like to be a contributor to the change-making movements.

Andres Pira is the author, with Dr. Joe Vitale, of the book, *Homeless to Billionaire: The 18 Principles of Wealth Attraction And Creating Unlimited Opportunity.* Becoming a millionaire at thirty was only the beginning for Swedish billionaire, entrepreneur, speaker, and author Andres Pira. At the age of 35, Pira went on to gain a net worth of that of a billionaire! Based in Phuket, Thailand, his group of companies under Blue Horizon Developments is currently a luxury resort empire of 19 companies with 249 employees and growing. A serial businessman, his portfolio spans real estate, gyms, a law office, a gas station, coffee shops, and a live events company. Blue Horizon Developments has received over fifteen awards from internationally acclaimed property awards groups such as International Property Awards, Thailand Property, and Dot Property Group. A philanthropist at heart, Pira believes one's true wealth is the good one does in this world. In his spare time, Pira enjoys mountain climbing, skydiving, bungee jumping, skiing, bodybuilding, and football. https://andrespira.com

* * * * * *

Let's talk about creating assets.

I write every day. I write non-fiction books, interactive workshops, speeches, videos, online courses, novels, and screenplays. I am constantly creating assets that are intellectual property.

Every month, I earn income from a major online retailer for my books and eBooks. I am also creating audio products. I earn money from my online courses with different hosts/services.

I am developing three entertainment franchises (that include novels, graphic novels, and upcoming filmed TV series). I have multiple entertainment projects.

Why? Because when you're pitching "in the room," in Hollywood, you need to respond well to the question, "What else do you got?" That's the classic question.

My focus is to be able to put things on the table including graphic novels, novels, and more.

Every month, I am earning income from work I did years ago.

What kind of assets will you create or build in your life? Will you purchase a property? Will you create intellectual property?

* * * * * *

Gamify Your Wealth
Principle #2
Keep track of the days in which you complete a vital task. Start with "1" and carry on through "103" and beyond. As the number gets higher, *you feel better* than simply checking off that the task is completed.

In recent years, I learned that watching the number rise gives me a boost of good energy. For example, I have given my sweetheart 807 daily foot massages (as of this writing). That's better than simply putting a check mark on that action each day. Placing a checkmark is like noting a chore was endured. **On the other hand, watching the number rise makes you feel like a champion.**

This is a prime part of using gamification. You get to feel in a way like a video games champion. This releases dopamine, a neurotransmitter that is part of the brain's reward pathway.

In days past, people typed their initials, Then, they were recognized as the top champion of a video game at the arcade.

Keep a Progress Log that reveals evidence that you *are* doing the work. *(Your Progress Log helps you add new data, change an old perception, and become fluid.)*

"If you can't fly, then run. If you can't run, then walk. If you can't walk, then crawl, but whatever you do, you have to keep moving." – Martin Luther King Jr.

* * * * * *

Gamify Grid #3 (Example)	
Action	Rehearse the beginning of a speech for 9 minutes in the morning before brushing one's teeth.
Token	Place a coin into a jar.
Date Start	11/22/20__
Date Completion	11/26/20__
Self-Reward	Have dinner at a favorite restaurant.

Now, it's your turn to fill out the Gamify Grid…

Gamify Grid	
Action	
Token	
Date Start	
Date Completion	
Self-Reward	

Important Point to Remember:
Build a relationship. Listen.

Power Question:
Will you ask a friend to help you practice listening attentively?

A side note: Many researchers and implementers of gamification emphasize "Create competition." Yes. That is often useful. You may note that in this book, I often focus on you rating your own score and achievements. Why? I emphasize: *Measure by your heart, not by others' approval.* From working with clients and students, I have noticed something valuable. People who measure their own achievements and get *satisfaction internally* demonstrate a specific and reliable power. **This is a *power to be independent* of outside reviews by others. This makes you strong.**

I say, "Be as strong as you can, as long as you can."

Another side note:
Gamify Your Wealth and Intrinsic Rewards

In many examples of the Gamify Grid, you will note extrinsic rewards like attending a movie theater and seeing a film. It would be ideal if many of the crucial wealth-building activities had the element of an intrinsic reward.

For something to have intrinsic value, it is interesting and satisfying on its own.

A problem is some wealth-building activities are merely a chore. Saving money can be a chore. Additionally, it can be a chore to refine your product offering so that it solves a Red-hot Burning Pain Point for a customer.

The Self-Determination Theory (Edward L. Deci, Richard Ryan, and others) holds that a human being has three psychological needs: autonomy, competence, and relatedness. Autonomy focuses on being the causal agent of your own life. Competence includes the experience of mastery of skills. Relatedness is about connecting and experiencing how you *care* for other people.

Gamification is about using human needs to inspire action.

Gamification also engages a human being's natural tendencies to take certain actions. This book emphasizes extrinsic rewards, yet it also holds space for the value of intrinsic rewards. For example, I write every day. I experience an intrinsic value in how I develop as a writer and as someone who serves audiences and readers.

If you choose to use an extrinsic reward (buying 3 songs on iTunes) where is the intrinsic part? I emphasize the intrinsic part is to make *the Big Choice.* You are choosing to expand wealth. Why? Perhaps, you want *peace of mind.* That's the intrinsic part. The use of gamification is in service of that benefit.

This book is *not* waiting for you to happen upon intrinsic value in certain wealth-building activities. When it is necessary, using extrinsic rewards is a practical process.

Chapter 4

Use the W.E.A.L.T.H. System
Work Your Confidence

(Create the "Skillful You")

We continue with the "C" of A.C.T.S.

Create the "Skillful You"

While writing this book, I did something I had never done before. I delivered a presentation at the Children of the Night International Dracula Congress (a conference). This was a stretch for me.

Why? Because my expertise is not the focus of these academics' work about Dracula.

How could I bring something relevant to those who devote so much of their life to that topic?

I began with my own authentic journey. My topic was "Writing Dracula: From Intimidated to Inspired."

How could I speak to academics and create rapport quickly? Without rapport, they might give resistance and miss the value I would bring to them.

How did I do it? I rehearsed in front of people who would give me valuable coaching. I put myself on "the hot seat." I risked looking foolish to people I respect and admire.

"Trying to be invulnerable makes us weak."
– Bob Choat

Pretending to be strong is *not* strength. **Strength rises from being coachable.**

What did I learn? I realized how to make an *immediate connection* with an audience of academics devoted to stories of Dracula.

How did I make an instant connection with the audience?

I quoted from the "sacred text"—the original Bram Stoker's *Dracula* novel. I talked about how I taught certain portions of the text to my college and graduate students at Academy of Art University.

My speech at this conference went well. I enjoyed answering the questions. I gave them insights into my process of writing my novel *Jenalee Storm: Against the House of Dracula* (under my pen name of Raven Aren James).

I believe in:

Rehearse. It frees you to improvise well in the moment.

Rehearse. It conditions you to do well in the clutch moment.*

* The clutch moment in basketball is when the player shoots and scores—or shoots and chokes. It's the moment of intense pressure.

I emphasize:

Courage is easier when you're prepared.

What skills do you need to develop?

Every day, I write and test my material. This is a similar process as a standup comedian improves their material.

"When I start a tour, it's not like I start out in arenas. Before this last tour, I performed in this place in New Brunswick called the Stress Factory. I did about 40 or 50 shows getting ready for the tour." – Chris Rock, top standup comedian

I recall the classic phrase: "The saxophone player must keep up their 'chops.'" This relates to the facial area. What this means is that a musician must keep physically fit and in practice so they can play music at the highest level.

* * * * * *

Gamify Your Wealth
Principle #3
Set up a good Gamify Pattern and you are trustworthy to yourself. Then, you are trustworthy to others. They want you to succeed.

Separate yourself from those individuals who live "lives of quiet desperation." Many people are stressed out, tired, and depleted. They break promises to themselves. They feel bad. And they cannot trust themselves. Instead, you can set up a well-formed Gamify Pattern. You can succeed at completing your daily action. Then you can trust yourself. This is an excellent foundation to build a great life.

* * * * * *

Gamify Grid #4 (Example)	
Action	Create a new skill by rehearsing it 9 minutes a day.
Token	Place a button in a jar.
Date Start	7/15/20__
Date Completion	7/29/20__
Self-Reward	Buy music that will send your spirit soaring.

Now, it's your turn to fill out the Gamify Grid…

Gamify Grid	
Action	
Token	
Date Start	
Date Completion	
Self-Reward	

* * * * * *

Now, we move to a view "behind the curtain" to see how gamification helps you create more wealth.

3 Big Ideas of Gamify Your Wealth

My science of Code Access Reset™ is focused on instant access of knowledge to be used in the clutch moment.

The clutch moment in a basketball game is when the player shoots and scores—or shoots and chokes.

The clutch moment is one of significant pressure and stress.

How can you remember something? If you boil it down to 3 Major Ideas, it is more memorable.

This is the reason why, using Code Access Reset™, I often keep ideas as three points embodied with one word.

Now, we'll look at 3 Big Ideas of Gamify Your Wealth.

Here is the N.O.W. System:

N – nothing like work
O – open a Progress Log for dopamine
W – wake up hope

1. Nothing like work.

Playing video games for many of us is nothing like work. How's that? Three things. One, you play. Two, it's your choice. Three, you enjoy getting better at the activity.

2. Open a Progress Log for dopamine.

When I say, "open a Progress Log," I mean *track your actions* in a Progress Log.

When you track a completed action in your Progress Log, you can stimulate the release of dopamine. It's a neural transmitter that is an essential part of the reward pathway in the brain. In other words, when you do something that can give you pleasure, the brain secretes dopamine that lights up the part of your brain. It feels like a reward. So, for many people, simply logging the completed action feels good--and feels like that reward.

Keeping a Progress Log may start as a form of discipline.

I often share…

"Only the disciplined ones are free in life." -- *Eliud Kipchoge*

Here I'll add:

People skilled in the release of dopamine can use the Power of Gamification so they excel.

How?

According to Dr. Anna Lembke, author of *Dopamine Nation,* the secretion of dopamine is the measurement of how addictive a behavior or drug is.

We noticed that the brain is structured to easily become addicted.

But what does "skilled in the release of dopamine" mean? It means you choose to do an action that is a "positive addiction."

"The positive addict enjoys his addiction, but it does not dominate his life. From it, he gains mental strength which he uses to help himself accomplish whatever he tries to do more successfully." – Dr. William Glasser

In this case, we're talking about using the Progress Log habit each night as a positive addiction. For several people, it can be something that releases dopamine.

Here's an example. When I was in college, I went to sleep each night *sad*. Why? I could never "win." Each night, I still had more studying to do. I worked at two jobs on campus: the campus mailroom and the science library. I studied for my double major.

After college, I developed a positive habit of my *Daily Power Page*. I log my progress. I have a good day every day. Yes, sometimes, I have terrible moments during the day. For example, I experience deep sadness when visiting my bedridden, 93-year-old mother. Due to my skills with humor, I can get her laughing. But her days are dreary because she is stuck in bed.

Still, I have good moments every day. And I know it because I log all the victories and blessings of each day.

Writing and building my intellectual properties comprise victories.

Talking with great friends is a true blessing.

I talk about *The One Choice.* The one choice that transforms addiction to elevation and life improvement.

Here is an example of **The One Choice: Use a Log to Feel Good As You Log Each Vital Task Completed.**

Log your behaviors.

Take advantage of feelings of accomplishment—and for several people—truly good feelings.

3. **Wake up hope.**

You can use a Progress Log to track every time you complete an effective action. **This act of tracking your progress can inspire hope in your heart.**

Over 20 years of developing my science of Code Access Reset™, I developed specific language. I focus on two types of hope. Action-Hope and Wishful-Hope. Many people like to indulge in Wishful-Hope. That is, they just sit there and wish for something positive to happen. Some time ago, some authors emphasized this popular phrase: "Act, Believe, Receive." That sounds nice.

However, several researchers and authors feel that something is missing in that phrase. The phrase might be more powerful in this form: "Ask, Believe, Take Lots of Effective Action, and Finally Receive."

So, when we talk about "wake up hope," we're talking about wake up Action-Hope. That's what this book is about. That's what *gamify your wealth* is truly expressing.

And what about hope? I developed my science of Code Access Reset™ in several settings. I've worked with thousands of MBA students, clients, and audience members. I have personally witnessed that hope can be comprised of four elements.

I say, "Hope can take a F.O.R.M."

Hope includes…

F – freedom

O – opportunity

R – realize fulfillment

M – meaning

"He who has a why to live for can bear almost any how."
– Friedrich Nietzsche

"Pleasure is about stimulating the senses. Happiness is found by being grateful for what I've got. Success is getting what I want. Fulfillment is giving what I've got." – Keith J. Cunningham

When you skillfully use your Progress Log, you open up a whole new level of living. You apply the skills of Gamify Your Wealth.

Important Point to Remember:

You can use a Progress Log to help you experience Action-Hope.

Power Question:

What vital action are you going to track in your Progress Log?

Some thoughts on Game Thinking

"I've worked on massive hit games that reached millions of people. Yet none of these games appeals to everyone. Stylistically, people seek out a wide variety of experiences. I enjoy Rock Band and Covet Fashion; my son prefers adrenaline-pumping shooters, and my best friend is addicted to candy-coated puzzlers. One person's beloved game is another's worst nightmare." – Amy Jo Kim

A comment: This book has examples of possible actions, tokens, and self-rewards. The questions I include invite you to customize your own thinking of how you will use gamification to accomplish tasks that will elevate your life.

"Successful games all have something in common: the intrinsic joy of skill-building. It feels good to engage our brains, improve our skills, and make progress along a path toward mastery." – Amy Jo Kim

A comment: I mention the work of Dr. Anna Lembke, author of *Dopamine Nation*. I encourage you to make a game out of doing what elevates your personal wealth. Why? With the right patterns, you can release dopamine (a neurotransmitter) and activate the reward pathway in your brain. Then, you elevate the likelihood that you will accomplish the tasks required for your prosperity.

"Game thinking is a framework for building products that make your customers more powerful, knowledgeable, and connected. Like lean startup, game thinking is grounded in testing assumptions. And like design thinking, we start out in a problem space (an unmet need) and end in a solution space (how your product fills

that need). Game Thinking extends these approaches with a disciplined, proven methodology for driving engagement by upgrading your customers—one of the most powerful and positive way to keep people coming back." – Amy Jo Kim

A comment: I have designed this book to cover essential topics for wealth creation and preservation. Lots of theory is beyond the scope of this book. For over 20 years, in applying my science of Code Access Reset™ with clients, graduate students, and audiences, I have streamlined my communications. I often say, "I write for business owners." This is a sleek way to say that I'm writing for people who want concise techniques so they can move forward now.

Why? As Amy Jo Kim mentions, we're "driving engagement."

About "testing assumptions": I invite you to try any technique in this book that captures your attention. Start small. My phrase is: Better than zero. Begin and build momentum.

Let's continue.

Chapter 5

Use the W.E.A.L.T.H. System Work Your Confidence

(Transform Bad Habits)

We continue with the "T" of A.C.T.S.

Transform Bad Habits

My friend, Max, tossed open a door at his workplace. He went through the doorway and didn't see the metal door on a cabinet left open. The edge of the metal door tore into his arm.

The wound later became infected.

Max saw a doctor. They got into a conversation about Max's smoking habit.

Being wounded changed Max's perspective. He felt vulnerable. Worse. Getting older, he noticed his wound took twice as long to heal.

What was smoking doing to his lungs?!

Realizing his vulnerability and that each day he was getting closer to death, he felt an urgency to quit smoking.

How could he make this new attempt at quitting smoking stick this time?

Here's a Big Crucial Principle: You don't drop bad habits. You must *transform* bad habits. How?

You must replace the bad habit.

Why? When you simply drop a bad habit, you leave a hole in your behavior patterns.

The easy thing is to fall back into the bad habit behavior.

Instead, you need a better strategy. Replace the behavior.

Use the T.O.P. System to Transform a Habit

T – tap into urgency
O – open to a Replacement Habit
P – place rewards

1. Tap into Urgency

When Max endured the infection on his arm, he felt the urgency of his vulnerability to health problems.

He then used that energy to find ways to ensure his release from smoking.

2. Open to a Replacement Habit

Instead of taking a smoking break, Max replaced it with a walking break.

At home, he took breaks by closing his eyes and listening to soothing music. He added deep breathing.

Here's an example of transforming a habit regarding shopping.

I transformed how I shop at a major online retailer's

website.

1) I do *not* buy items late at night when I am solo.
2) I talk through the purchase with my sweetheart. She may have some comments. And she serves as my "accountability partner" so we stay on track with our financial goals.

How will you transform a bad habit you have?

3. Place rewards

One can use tokens to earn a reward.

Here's an example. Mia wants a new album of music.

She designates one token for each day she is free of smoking. Mia chooses to give herself the reward of a new album of music after 7 days smoke-free. She has placed seven tokens into a jar. Each day she sees her progress.

Here's another example. I use a "Mini-Reward."

I experience good feelings with my Mini-Reward when I log my progress on a *Daily Power Page*. I track my exercise. When I added weight training to my weekly pattern, I noted each session completed. At the time of this writing, I have completed 209 sessions. Each time I write down a number representing a daily completed session, I experience a good feeling.

Writing down the number 209 served as a Mini-Reward of a good feeling.

Each step forward inspires hope in my heart.

Here's another example.

I track my writing.

Here is a Daily Power Page entry:

Day 5: 11/18 10 min. 2072 words end 11:47 PM

"2072 words" refers to the total number of words written for that book up to the end of Day 5.

On that particular day, I only devoted 10 minutes to writing. But I encouraged myself by saying, **"Better than zero."**

On other days, I dictate 355 words in 20 minutes.

A reward can be a good feeling one gets upon accomplishing a small step forward.

* * * * * *

Replace Procrastination by using the Power of the *10-Minute Timer Reset*

Every week, I face moments when I feel that starting a writing session is a horrible chore. I'm tired. Sometimes, it is 11 pm after a vigorous day.

I replace the urge to procrastinate by setting a timer and writing for 10 minutes. I tell myself, "Just 10 minutes, that will be enough for tonight. *Better than zero.*" I end up resetting the timer, so I accomplish writing for 80 minutes.

This may sound silly. But it is based on acknowledging discoveries by researchers focused on psychology. My degree is in psychology.

To start writing can be hard. Why? You must pass through doubt, inertia, and procrastination. The hard part is crossing the threshold.

"The scariest moment is always just before you start. After that, things can only get better." – Stephen King

This *10-Minute Timer Reset Method* can be applied to many tough tasks, including doing one's tax paperwork preparation.

* * * * * *

Gamify Your Wealth
Principle #4
Set an easy, simple task to get started, gain momentum, and elevate your morale.

Some people set their sights too high and then crash and burn. Instead, pick something that you are sure you can do. For example, Sandra began practicing martial arts. She set a plan to do 10 motions of a certain kick (five per leg). She also did 10 motions of another form of kick. That's only 20 motions and that takes less than 1 minute. Sandra can easily add that to her day. As she successfully changes her days, she gains momentum. This energizes her and elevates her mood.

* * * * * *

Gamify Grid #5 (Example)	
Action	Do ten sit-ups per day
Token	One coin. Place it into a jar.
Date Start	11/22/20__
Date Completion	11/2620__
Self-Reward	Take a luxurious bath for one hour. Read a favorite book.

Now, it's your turn to fill out the Gamify Grid…

Gamify Grid	
Action	
Token	
Date Start	
Date Completion	
Self-Reward	

Important Point to Remember:

It's better when you transform a bad habit instead of merely dropping it.

Power Questions:

What habit do you want to remove from your daily life? How will you transform this habit?

Chapter 6

Use the W.E.A.L.T.H. System
Work Your Confidence

(Set "this month better than last month")

We continue with the "S" of A.C.T.S.

Set "this month better than last month"

Emma, one of my clients, landed a $12,000 client. How? She gave in-person workshops that led to gaining her clients.

Then the Covid-19 pandemic hit, and she lost her whole marketing model.

She moved into other ways to earn money. But she felt devastated that her supposed big life change came crashing down.

At one point, when coaching her, I said, "Are you doing better this month than last month?"

"Yes, " she said.

"And are you developing new ways to bring in more

income?"

She nodded.

"How's that feel?"

"Okay. It feels better," she said, with a smile.

How will you set "this month better than last month"?

Are you developing assets?

Here are possible assets:

- Property/real estate
- books
- speeches
- online courses
- graphic novels
- screenplays
- workout program you can use to coach people
- and more

What assets do you want to develop?

Are you gaining valuable training*?

I invite you to celebrate. You're gaining training with this book at this moment. Congratulations on your efforts with this book.

*** I offer other forms of training:**

- Videos/Podcast Episodes – Succeed Even If
- Online Courses

At GetTheBigYES.com/courses

- Audio books/eBooks/paperback books at a major online retailer's website
- Interactive Workshops – GetTheBigYES.com

What training are you going to enroll in?

To expand your wealth, think of how you can upsell. That means, someone comes into your world—perhaps, through a free video on YouTube or other form of social media. They can purchase an audio program, move up to (an upsell) an online course—and then, perhaps, attend one of your in-person training events.

If you are selling products, an upsell can follow this pattern. The person buys a pet collar and then purchases a pet bed.

To Set a Better Month, Have Support from the Right People in Your Life

Here is an interview with David Chametzky, the Deep Message Expert, Growth Coach, TEDx Speaker, Producer, and Media Host. We now explore the power of friendship.

Interview with David Chametzky

Tom: Dave, there is so much you can share from your wisdom and experience. You came back from a "bottom space." You were in a space where you nearly took your own life. When you came back from that, what in your life has really been a blessing?

David: The blessing really has been friendship. The friends I have. At that time, in the first moments of trying to put my life back together, I appreciated the people who were there for me—who held me when I didn't want to be held. They lifted me up when I couldn't be lifted up—because I didn't want to be.

... Who I am now is not the same person I was four years ago—when that happened.

A lot of growth came in. I thank the people who saved my life. Not physically, I made choices. But they supported me. They made sure I took a breath every day—even though I didn't want to.

There are a lot of people who made me think of how blessed I am. The blessings are among the things I'm really grateful for.

Tom: I'm with you. ... I have a phrase: "If you don't have a reserve now, how can you handle more?"

Over the four years, would you call it a recovery?

David: Yeah. I call it a *Rise.* It was definitely a recovery from the thinking that I did. I don't know if I would focus on "reserve." **It's using your resources properly.** It comes down to how do we "redirect?" How do we release the burdens?

... At that time, I felt that I knew all the answers. That I could do it myself. I had the disease that many of us have: "I know that already." But until you do it, it doesn't matter that you "know it." You can read a book and still not understand the thing.

We need to be careful about the ego.

Ego is about trying to protect ourselves... You need to keep it in check. If you feed the ego too much, it's like eating too much of one thing. It might not be healthy.

It's about being a lion tamer. Knowing the lion and having the ability to manage the lion. It's the same thing with ego. Just make sure you don't get bitten.

Tom: I hear you. I imagine that you now have a different relationship with your ego.

David: For sure. For example, last December, I published my first book. I was lucky enough to have my book show up in Times Square (New York). For a New Yorker, it's amazing to have your book shown on an electronic billboard—in Times Square.

Tom: Yes!

David: The holiday rush. It was the middle of December. I needed to make sure that my ego was kept in check. It wasn't like "Oh, look at me!" If anything, I tempered my enthusiasm a bit because I wanted to keep my ego in check. It's not about me. And it's not about how my book is the most wonderful thing in the world. How I did that was to look around Times Square. There were thousands of people there. Even though my picture was next to Patrick Mahomes who is a football player well-known by millions. People weren't paying attention. They were just going about their business. I used that as an opportunity to remind myself that this is good for me. And I felt very good. Holding my book sends energy through me. But in the grand scheme of things, people weren't paying attention.

Tom: I'm with you. I flow with what you're saying. I came up with the phrase: "Expression is the celebration." I celebrate that there was something to be born from you. You did everything you needed to do. The book is now in the world. ... I think that a lot of people don't celebrate until they get something that feeds the ego.

David: A lot of people do. I put myself in check. I ask, "What am I doing this for?"

Tom: So, if you were going to express a Miracle Secret, what would that be? This is the wisdom you would give to your daughters and the next generation.

David: Do as many things as you can that would feed your soul—not the ego.

Do the things that would make you happy. Don't worry about anyone else. Just take care of yourself. And keep your eyes on the prize. Keep growing. Those are the Miracle Secrets that everyone knows but not many do. Because they feel that they 'know this so well.' ***But you need to apply it. Not just "know it."***

David Chametzky, known as the Deep Message Expert, is a Producer, Author, Media Host, Growth Coach, Mentor, and Philanthropist. He is the author of *When Your Heart Says "It's Time to Soar!"*

He is the Producer of the Coaching and Mentoring Curriculum to assist you in finding *Time to Soar* on your path to finding Resources for Empowering Personal Growth. He leads resilience programs.

David Chametzky is the Media Host of the high-ranking Podcast "Peace Love & Bring A Bat."

His Podcasts and programs help people rise to higher levels of living and succeeding. They soar as they are *On the Path*.

Following his heart for philanthropic community support, David Chametzky co-founded the organization Goons For Good, serving people who need hope and resources. See DavidChametzky.com

* * * * * *

Gamify Your Wealth
Principle #5
When you complete your actions and log them, be careful about your conversations. Carefully choose who you will talk to and share your new experiences. Why? Some people are energy-drainers. Instead, you need to stay strong. Guard your energy and resolve.

When you begin a new behavior pattern, it's new and vulnerable. Many individuals are easily talked out of doing something new. I have an elderly relative who often says, "That's not normal." Really? *To live a life of joy and adventure may not be "normal," but it is worth doing.* I am careful to avoid bringing a new idea to this particular relative. I call that "the place where new ideas go to die." Similarly, I invite you to carefully choose who you talk to. Avoid the energy-drainers. Keep yourself strong.

* * * * * *

Gamify Grid #5 (Example)	
Action	Rehearse the opening of a speech with four different friends ... one on each consecutive day.
Token	Place jellybeans in a jar.
Date Start	6/03/20__
Date Completion	6/07/20__
Self-Reward	Go to the movie theater with a friend and enjoy a film.

Now, it's your turn to fill out the Gamify Grid…

Gamify Grid	
Action	
Token	
Date Start	
Date Completion	
Self-Reward	

Important Point to Remember:
To excel, have support from the right people in your life.

Power Questions:
Who really has your back? Who do you trust?

Chapter 7

Use the W.E.A.L.T.H System Elevate Your Influence (Part 1)

I'm auditioning for a commercial. I'm scared. It's a new experience for me.

Critical eyes are on me. The director in the center. The producer is to his right. And another person to his left.

I complete reciting words from the script.

But then, these words flow from my mouth:

"Are you going to say *Yes* to having me in your commercial?"

A moment. Nothing happens. Then the director nods. I'm nodding. He looks to the producer. She nods.

"Tom, you're in our commercial," the director says.

And I learn the power of putting "yes" into the room.

This is the power of...
"Are you going to say Yes to...?"

Years later, I'm on the phone with the leader of a sales team (a company in New York).

I say, "Are you going to say Yes to having me join your team?"

Silence.

Then…

"Yes. You'll start right away," the leader says.

I close this sale—to get the position—in one phone call.

Closing this sale in one phone call includes two more details.

1) I had a powerful referral to get the opportunity to call this leader.
2) I spoke confidently with evidence of my past sales performances.*

** My phrase (repeated in this book) is **Confidence is built on evidence. Prepare, and you know you have an advantage.***

How did I get a powerful referral that led to my closing a sale in one phone call?

I learned how to get people to want to see me succeed.

Get People to Want to See You Succeed

What if you could get people to want to see you succeed? I know this is possible because when I started in the film industry it was about good relationships.

I had a good relationship with a software engineer who sent my first screenplay to another software engineer. The second person passed my screenplay forward to a real estate developer. Then, that man gave my screenplay to the

California Motion Picture Commissioner Dewitt Ladd Rucker. He gained, for my first feature film, two vital elements. San Luis Obispo Airport and an American Eagle airplane. Both were free.

Now I share crucial methods.

We use the M.E.E.T.S. System:

M – meet with ease and smiles
E – engage specifics they care about
E – express you're coachable – and you listen
T – take their "take"
S – support them in the way they prefer

1. Meet with ease and smiles.

When someone new meets you, they don't like feeling uncomfortable. So, it's crucial that you put them at ease. Often, we can do well by having a gentle smile. But don't leave it on your face too long. Or it may come across as phony. People who know who they are and have confidence, smile. Then the smile naturally fades away when appropriate.

If you're not used to smiling, practicing a bit helps.

2. Engage specifics they care about.

How can you find out what is important to another person? You can ask, "What's most important to you about...?"

It's important to listen carefully. Then say back specific details you learn as the conversation continues. When you say back what you heard, you demonstrate that you truly listened. This puts the person at ease and gives them some joyful moments. *Someone is listening to me.*

My sweetheart taught me to avoid just asking general questions like: "So what are you looking forward to?" Instead, one can ask, "So how is your dog, Gertrude, doing after the surgery?" Specifics are crucial. Make sure to focus on what the other person cares about.

3. Express you're coachable—and you listen.

When I teach the course, *Convince Investors to Fund You,* I emphasize that people can trust you if you are coachable. I have a relative who never listens, who never admits any mistakes, and more. I cannot trust this person. They are *not* coachable. They don't care enough to want to get better at anything. They're done. They think they've learned all they need to learn. They feel there's nothing more to explore or to improve in life. It's tragic really.

Instead, you and I can strive to be coachable and to listen to people. Then life is a continuous adventure. Every day you learn something.

4. Take their "take."

Here is something powerful. Ask a person, "So what is your take on this?" A take is often built on someone's experience or even some data.

In Silicon Valley, California where I live, I talk to advisors who are keeping up with what's going on. They are experts in their fields. I learn every day. I ask them, "So what's your take on this?

I often say, "I prefer to hold perceptions. Give me new data and I can quickly change a perception."

On the other hand, several people hold to their opinions. It appears that they would sweat blood if they were called upon to change their opinion. Why? The opinion is tied to their identity. It hurts too much to change.

When you stay curious, flexible, and open to learning, people can trust you.

Remember to ask, "So, what is your take on this...?"

5. **Support them in the way they prefer.**

In my circle, when appropriate, I ask a person, "So, how can I support you in the way you prefer?"

A particular writer-director makes films in which the dialogue is off. However, if their friend said, "Hey man, you need to improve your dialogue," that friend might lose the friendship.

On the other hand, when someone asked me for feedback I asked them, "Is there some area that you're concerned about?"

In this way, I avoid saying anything that's not relevant. My interest is: Support the relationship and maintain rapport.

That's the reason that I often say, "How can I support you in the way you prefer?"

I also say, "I have a response. *It's just clay for the table.* If you like it, you can shape it. If it doesn't fit, you can scrape it off the table. Shape it or scrape it."

My point with saying "clay for the table" is that I demonstrate that my ego is *not* attached to the observation I made.

When you use the techniques of the M.E.E.T.S. system, you are creating a circle of associates and friends *who want to see you succeed.* This is an essential element of my work, *Elevate Your Influence.*

I interviewed Danielle Strachman, a cofounder and

general partner of 1517 Fund, a top-tier pre-seed fund. She discussed important concerns when building a business relationship.

Interview with Danielle Strachman

A portion of the interview…

Tom: What is a mistake that one might make when building a new relationship with an investor?

Danielle: Going back to what you [Tom] said about trust. One of the meta-things we look at is how a founder drives the process if they're looking to close out in a week or a month.

For example, we had a team that we went into diligence with. This team was working on a very interesting problem. Due diligence was going great. We did a customer call—that was wonderful.

Everything was wonderful except for this one piece, which was how the founders were interacting with us to do the sale of their company. The founders were really driving things, using FOMO [fear of missing out] tactics. They said, "Hey, if we don't hear from you by Friday, we're going to have this term sheet from somebody else."

At our stage, the pre-seed stage, somebody else might set terms. But it's not like a Series A Round when somebody takes 80% of the round, and it's over. At this stage, the checks are more collaborative. People are coming in for 10% or maybe 15% of the company at most. We're working with smaller amounts of capital. The risk appetite is high, but you also have to distribute that risk.

When we have had founders, who had sales that were not genuine and their approach was based on manipulative techniques, we said *no.*

We'll go back to the example of the team that had one piece that caused trouble. I returned to that team, and I wrote a long piece of feedback: "Listen. I really liked everything. But one thing that has really put us in the No camp was your leadership ability and your ability to walk us through this process. Because one of our core beliefs is how people are in one context is how they are in all contexts."

So, if the person is using spammy, infomercial techniques like "act now"—everything is fast—that's probably how they will treat their employees, how they work with customers, and things like that. We look at the situation from a higher bird's eye level of "Would we want them doing this with other people as well?"

I said to the team, "It would have been authentic for us to hear something that is really happening. Maybe you have an engineer that you want to hire and if you don't close by Friday, you're going to lose out on that person."

There *is* real pressure that happens in this business. But I'd rather hear about that, instead of FOMO tactics to get us interested. I'd rather build our relationship up based on what you really need, not from smoke-and-mirrors and fakeness. **So, that's a big mistake that people will make: Their sales process isn't authentic.**

Danielle Strachman is a venture capitalist, entrepreneur, and philanthropist. She is the founder and general partner of the 1517 Fund and founder of a project-based learning charter school called the Innovations Academy.

Danielle Strachman is also a Thiel Fellowship alumna. Since graduating from the program, she has been involved with alternative education. She intends to disrupt the education sector while helping young entrepreneurs.(from Everipedia.org)

* * * * * *

Gamify Your Wealth
Principle #6
When creating a new habit that feels like a strain … create a positive "welcome." This means you add something to lessen the pain involved. For example, many people find it helpful to listen to good music at the start of a writing session.

A positive "welcome" is an experience that takes the sting out of starting a tough task.

You can listen to good music. You could sip warm and flavorful tea. Or perhaps, you have a favorite cup of soda that you enjoy. Create your own positive "welcome" and get started.

It's important to have a process or pattern that reliably gets you into action.

"The secret of getting ahead is getting started. The secret of getting started is breaking your complex overwhelming tasks into small manageable tasks, and then starting on the first one."
– Mark Twain

"The really happy people are those who have broken the chains of procrastination, those who find satisfaction in doing the job at hand. They're full of eagerness, zest, productivity. You can be, too." – Norman Vincent Peale

"A professional is someone who can do his best work when he doesn't feel like it." – Alistair Cooke

* * * * * *

Gamify Grid #6 (Example)	
Action	Do some daily reading about how to better run your business (or communicate more effectively at work).
Token	Place a bottle cap into a small box.
Date Start	1/9/20__
Date Completion	1/18/20__
Self-Reward	Enjoy your morning cup of coffee.

Now, it's your turn to fill out the Gamify Grid…

Gamify Grid	
Action	
Token	
Date Start	
Date Completion	
Self-Reward	

Important Point to Remember:

Create a positive "welcome" so you take some pain out of starting your chosen daily action.

Power Question:

What are you going to use as your positive "welcome" at the start of your daily action?

Congratulations on your progress. Here is

Your Free Reward → See this Free Video:

Protect Yourself from Poisoners of Your Wealth

By Tom Marcoux

Go to: http://GetTheBigYES.com/protect_yourself

This video is from

Chapter 8

Use the W.E.A.L.T.H. System Elevate Your Influence (Part 2)

(Avoid Mistakes that Make People Label You an Amateur)

Daniel could feel it. This was the moment. This prospective client would hire him for his coaching program. This meant thousands of dollars in Daniel's pocket. Or nothing.

"You're sure, you can help me hit those income goals?" Joe, the prospective client asked.

But Daniel choked in the clutch moment.

There was a bit of hesitation.

Daniel lost the sale.

It was an amateur move.

Daniel became my client and told me about his crash and burn.

"Two things," I began. "First, the client wants two things from you: **hope and certainty**."

I continued, "Second, we can get you to the certainty. But you need to rehearse. We'll use my system of *Directed-Rehearsal.* In this moment, your body has some self-defeating behaviors. We will use my science Code Access Reset™. We'll condition you to be authentic, certain, and confident in the moment."

Daniel smiled. He knew he had the right coach with the system he needed to excel.

This section relates to how you can convince investors to fund your project. But it's more than that. People invest in you all the time. Just talking to you is an investment of time and energy.

Use the techniques in this section to develop a form of useful charisma.

To demonstrate confidence, you can often excel by subtly leading a conversation.

We use the L.E.A.D. system:

L – listen
E – engage in "Catch and Pivot"
A – acknowledge
D – deliver the truth

1. Listen

In my interactive workshop, *Convince Investors to Fund You,* I emphasize that investors continually test and push those people who are seeking funding. They want to know if you are a good leader—someone worth investing in. Or should they dismiss you?

Good leaders listen. Good leaders do *not* punish people

who tell them the truth. Good leaders maintain their calm when people give them opposition or difficult feedback.

While listening, a good leader can say, "I'm glad you brought that up..."

2. Engage in "Catch and Pivot"

The sentence, "I'm glad you brought that up" is part of what I call the "Catch" technique. It's like someone tossed you a ball, and you catch the ball.

I teach entrepreneurs how to come across as professionals and avoid mistakes that have investors label them as amateurs. I have them practice during the workshop in real-time. They learn how to do "Catch and Pivot."

This is how it sounds:

An Investor: "How could you even think to do that? Don't you know that XY has already destroyed that part of the market?"

An Entrepreneur uses the Catch technique: "I'm glad you shared that. That is an important consideration."

An Entrepreneur uses the Pivot technique: "I'm curious. Do you have a take on what is the most important thing to focus on—with the XY situation?"

3. Acknowledge

When an entrepreneur is in a tough meeting with potential high-value investors, the entrepreneur still needs to demonstrate leadership. One powerful technique to demonstrate leadership is to *acknowledge.*

In my interactive workshop, *Convince Investors to Fund You,* I have attendees practice saying something like, "Sarah, that's an important point. I'm glad you mentioned that."

By saying "That's an important point," you are *praising* the investor Sarah in this situation.

Acknowledging and praising are effective in getting someone on your side.

4. Deliver the truth.

Rehearse so you radiate confidence. Additionally, you'll enjoy moments of actually feeling confident.

Rehearse well and you can concisely deliver the truth.

During my workshops, I help founders of new companies focus on the most important details that investors care about.

I make it easy to remember. I say get paid. The word *paid* refers to four details that comprise the Big Idea.

Venture capitalists are focused on the Big Idea. I know because I have interviewed a number of them.

When a startup company leader pitches to a room of investors, they must express the Big Idea early in their presentation.

Here's how it is easy to remember what the Big Idea is:

Use the P.A.I.D. System:

P – profit
A – advantage
I – innovation
D – disruption

What kind of profit? Big profits. What kind of advantage? In Silicon Valley, California where I live, people talk of the *unfair advantage.* They are not looking for an incremental improvement.

It is crucial to know that rehearsal will help you deliver the truth in a smooth, confident, and trustworthy manner. This is part of how you get people to say yes to you.

* * * * * *

Elevate Your Influence

I interviewed Bill Reichert, a wise venture capitalist. He revealed some secrets of pitching and communicating effectively.

Interview with Bill Reichert

Tom: When somebody makes a pitch, what is crucial for them to do? What must they do positively?

Bill: In order to be effective at pitching, you've got to do three things. And you've got to do them in 20 seconds. First, you've got to be clear about what it is that your business is doing. The investor has to understand your business, your service or product. You have roughly one sentence to *clearly* communicate what business you're in.

Second, you have to be *compelling*. You have to get them to say, "Wow! That's amazing. Tell me more!" There has to be something about what you are doing that is incredibly exciting, that makes you stand out, that will cause your customers to love you. And you have to get this across in one or two sentences.

Third, you've got to be *credible.* There are a whole bunch of ways to communicate credibility. What is the indication that what you're telling me is true?... you're not just blowing smoke. One of the best is some level of third-party validation.

This brand name person or company is a customer or a partner. Convince the investor that you're really different than the alternatives; you're not just more of the same.

You've got to be clear, compelling, and credible in the first 20 seconds. Then investors will listen to the rest of your pitch, rather than checking their iPhones.

Tom: What is the big mistake that someone, who is delivering a pitch, must avoid?

Bill: The big mistake is doing the opposite of clear, compelling, and credible. And we see it all the time. It broadly fits into the category of *the curse of knowledge.* One VC calls it, "the paradox of brilliance." This is a nice way of saying it. Entrepreneurs live and breathe their product, market, and business all the time. As a result, it's sometimes hard for them to appreciate what the person on the other end, the investor, does *not* understand about what the entrepreneur is doing.

A classic example is the entrepreneur who says, "We're going to disrupt the entire home mortgage industry."

There's no content in that statement. This entrepreneur knows what they're doing and is probably excited about it. We know the company is doing something in the home mortgage industry. But we have no idea why *we* should be excited.

The entrepreneur goes on: "Our SaaS platform will transform the industry by automating manual processes and applying AI-based analytics." Intuitively, we get that automation and AI should be good things, but we still don't understand how this is going to transform and disrupt the industry. For whatever reason, entrepreneurs don't appreciate that we don't already know why their company is brilliant. This is a common, broad-based problem: Lack of clarity about what the heck you're doing. I can't tell you how many times I've been a judge at a pitch competition, and, after a four-minute pitch, one of the judges says, "I don't understand what your business is."

Another classic example of this problem is when an entrepreneur starts using jargon or acronyms to describe what they're doing. If you don't know what the acronym means, then you're totally lost.

Here's an example I love. An entrepreneur came in and said, "And unlike any other power electronics device company, we're using *silicon nitride!*" They looked at us like "Isn't that awesome—amazing—incredible?!"

The entrepreneur could not understand our lack of excitement. It was like they were thinking, *Why aren't you jumping up and down and screaming—and pouring money on us because we're using silicon nitride?!*

The entrepreneur did not understand that we didn't appreciate the extraordinarily compelling physics of their technology. This is an inability to bridge the gap between the entrepreneur's expertise and where the audience is. The entrepreneur needs to communicate an understanding of why a novel technology can be the basis of a business or why a particular business model will be compelling to their customers. The entrepreneur needs to understand where the listener is and bridge the knowledge.

A related difficulty in pitching is that entrepreneurs may be used to pitching to prospective customers, but VCs are not prospective customers. VCs generally don't appreciate the needs the customers have and the context that the customers live in. If you don't make that context clear to investors, they may not appreciate why what you're doing is compelling.

Tom: Knowing what you know now, what would you have done differently?

Bill: (chuckles) I would have bought Tesla. I had the

opportunity to be in Tesla very early—before Elon Musk took over. A friend of mine, Nancy Pfund [founder and managing partner of DBL Partners], was trying to convince me why Tesla made sense for a small fund like ours. And I was trying to convince her that she was insane. That this was ludicrous, as a small fund, investing in a car company. She invested, and I didn't. She wound up with Model S number 2, and I didn't.

[Bill and Tom laugh.]

Bill: Another one that I didn't invest in was Lyft—before it was called Lyft. I sat down with John Zimmer, who pitched me on Zimride, and we passed on that.

That's in response to your phrasing of the question "knowing what you know now."

Tom: I'll ask a follow-up. What is more of a life lesson for someone who wants to excel and who wants to make an impact?

Bill: Now we're into the baring your soul part of the interview.

Tom: But I'm not Barbara Walters, so you don't have to cry.

[Bill laughs.]

Bill: One of my big life lessons has been to learn when to pick your fights. When I was a callow youth, I spent more time being urgent about asserting what I considered to be the right way or the truth.

I realized by being so urgent and pushing people harder than they, perhaps, wanted to be pushed, I pushed people away—when I didn't need to ... when it wasn't worth the fight. It wasn't worth being right.

This is the lesson that young high achievers need to learn. Because we're brought up in our culture and our educational system to always be right. The educational system puts this ultra-high premium on being right.

Then you're put into the work world where it's really hard to know what is right, but you still have this overachiever/high achiever ethic that *I got to be right.*

This *I got to be right* ethic slowed me down in a few situations.

Finally, I learned, "Hey Bill, you don't always have to be right." And you don't always have to fight for what you think is the right answer. Sometimes, it's not worth the fight. And, guess what, sometimes you're n. right. But in school, high achievers learn that "I don't know" is not an acceptable answer. In school, you have to always be right. The educational system focuses on individual achievement and punishes mistakes. It teaches students that there is a defined process for getting it right—for getting a good grade or a good score. But the real world doesn't work that way. The educational system damages our ability to engage in collaborative teamwork and think out of the box.

So, I've learned to pick my fights and how to collaborate better.

Bill Reichert is co-founder of Garage Technology Ventures, a seed and early-stage venture capital firm based in Silicon Valley. He is also a Partner at Pegasus Tech Ventures, a global venture capital firm with offices in Silicon Valley and around the world.

Bill and his partners invest in promising emerging technology companies and work intensively with them to help them grow and succeed. Some of Garage's most successful investments include Pandora Media (NYSE: P), Digital Fountain (acquired by Qualcomm), Coremetrics (acquired by IBM), iNest (acquired by LendingTree), and LeftHand Networks (acquired by HP).

Bill brings experience as a serial entrepreneur to his work with portfolio companies. Prior to co-founding Garage in 1998, Bill was co-founder of Academic Systems, a software company funded by Kleiner Perkins, Accel Partners, and Microsoft. Academic Systems became the leading developer of network-based interactive instructional materials for colleges and universities and was acquired by Plato Learning after an IPO. Prior to Academic Systems, Bill was a senior executive at several venture-backed technology companies, including The Learning Company, which was the leading developer of educational software in the United States before its acquisition in 1994, and Infa Technologies, a touchscreen computer company that developed many of the concepts underlying the Newton, Palm, and iPhone devices. Bill also co-founded Trademark Software, which was subsequently acquired by Dow Jones, while in graduate school at Stanford.

Earlier in his career, Bill worked for McKinsey & Co. in Los Angeles, the World Bank in Washington, DC, and Brown Brothers Harriman & Co., in New York. He has authored and co-authored several articles and speeches on entrepreneurship, venture capital, international trade, and monetary policy.

Bill earned his BA in History and Science from Harvard University and his MBA from Stanford University. He is a member of the Council on Foreign Relations in New York and is a former Chairman of the Churchill Club in Silicon Valley. He is also an Advisor to the Women's Startup Lab,

Nordic Innovation House, and the Korea Innovation Center. He lives with his extraordinary wife Michelle and three incredible children in Los Altos, California. You can contact Bill through Pegasus Tech Ventures.

* * * * * *

Gamify Your Wealth

Principle #7

If the action is boring, say, "It's just work." You let go of expectations.

How can you become effective and "elevate your influence"? You rehearse. A lot.

"Choose a job you love, and you'll never have to work a day in your life" – ascribed to Confucius

Is this true? Not in my life. I have had to work at everything that has been important to me.

I have served as a feature film director, novelist, guest lecturer at Stanford University, and more. Each role required work. I call it "good work." But each job has unpleasant parts. When I say, "It's just work," I change my expectations. I get into a state of being known as *acceptance.* I accept that I just need to work. For example, putting corrections in one's novel or non-fiction book is "just work." But it's worth it.

* * * * * *

Gamify Grid #7 (Example)	
Action	Rehearse your answers to two tough job interview questions.
Token	Place a jellybean into a jar.
Date Start	7/9/20__
Date Completion	7/19/20__
Self-Reward	Audiobook

Now, it's your turn…

Gamify Grid	
Action	
Token	
Date Start	
Date Completion	
Self-Reward	

Important Point to Remember:

The Big Idea is P.A.I.D. … Profit, Advantage, Innovation, and Disruption.

Power Question:

How will you prepare and rehearse so you communicate a Big Idea briefly—and in a compelling way?

Chapter 9

Use the W.E.A.L.T.H. System Elevate Your Influence (Part 3)

My first-time addressing Stanford University MBA students… my heart was racing.

The people who hired me warned me that these MBA students could be truly skeptical.

But I knew something. On a deeper level than merely an intellectual exercise.

You see, I started as a timid, shy, 9-year-old playing the piano in front of 31 seniors at a retirement facility (as I mentioned earlier in this book).

Why was I so scared playing piano for the seniors? I was focused on "How am I doing? Oh, not good enough. You're judging me."

Over years of training and experience, I learned to shift from "How am I doing?" to *How are YOU doing?"*

I am here to serve you. I am authentically serving you.

So that's what I knew on a deep level: Stay in the space

of *How are YOU doing?*

In front of the Stanford University MBA students, I *focused on* serving the students. That authentic intention empowered me. I took in a deep breath and said, "How many of us in this room, really want to create....?"

* * * * * *

I interviewed Natalie Glebova, empowerment coach, author, and former Miss Universe. She revealed insights about coming across with confidence and authenticity. Her suggestions are valuable when building relationships.

Interview with Natalie Glebova

Tom: To come across as confident and trustworthy, what does a person need to do?

Natalie: On a more spiritual level, I would say that in order to be confident and trustworthy, *be authentic.* That's the number one important thing.

The common cliché is to "be yourself." But what does this really mean? Being yourself means being present with yourself and being present with this moment.

You're being in touch with your body and in touch with your emotions. Don't let the thoughts overtake you. Feel the true essence of who you are. By focusing on your breathing and feeling the life inside of your body, you can experience and feel what it is like to be overtaken and to surrender to the present moment.

I believe that this is the key to appearing authentic and to convey your truth to other people. So, whatever you say comes from a place *not* driven by your ego. It's not driven by some concepts in your mind. But it's from a true place within yourself. That's the number one thing I recommend.

Tom: To appear confident and trustworthy, what is best for someone to *avoid?*

Natalie: Pay attention to your body language. Don't fidget. Don't play with your hands.

Instead of appearing like you're nervous, be still and be calm. Place your hands firmly on the table or at your sides as you *avoid* doing something constantly with your hands.

This is important because when people see you fidgeting, they get this feeling that you are nervous—or maybe you're trying to hide something. You seem *not* confident and that you're not really being yourself.

Tom: I have a follow-up question. There are people I talk with—someone comes up to me after I give a speech, and I would tell them the truth that you shared, *be yourself.* And, they would say, "This self? This nervous self I have? This scared self. If I was just tuned into the scared part of myself, then I don't think I could convince anyone of anything." So how do you make a shift to the true self?

Natalie: It doesn't happen overnight. In very rare cases you might be able to make a shift like a giant quantum leap from one mindset to another. It usually comes from experience and a lot of inner work. It comes with time, I believe.

But you can't just say, "I'm going to give it time." You have to actually do something in order to change your mindset and change the way you behave. So, you can write a list of things that scare you and journal about them to understand your feelings.

It helps to meditate every single day and visualize yourself as how you want to conduct yourself—in a public setting—a speech or a small group at your work or social circle.

A lot of deep introspection is needed to understand one's fear about how people are perceiving you or judging you. That's why I recommend journaling about your feelings to let them out. You can acknowledge that they're there, and then you meditate on that feeling. Every day meditate at least for 10 to 15 minutes—more if you can. I recommend 30 minutes. Observe your thoughts and feelings about the situation. Just allow them to be—before you release them.

You pay attention to your feelings, and you actually acknowledge them without judging them. You feel them. What is this tightness in my chest or anxiety feeling in the pit of my stomach? Watch yourself become aware of that feeling, and it will dissolve. Whenever I'm anxious about something, I close my eyes and I go deep down into the feeling—and when I am conscious of it without any judgment and observe it—it quickly disappears on its own.

You have to meditate and do introspective work on yourself every day. Then put yourself out there into the situations that make you uncomfortable. Because the only way to grow is to put yourself out of your comfort zone to experience new things firsthand.

Tom: Knowing what you know now, what would you have done differently?

Natalie: I was shy when I was younger. At 13, I arrived as a Russian immigrant in Canada. I had the lowest self-esteem.

Knowing what I know now if I could talk to my younger self, I would say,

"Always look for a different perspective. Any opinion

you have of yourself or someone else, there is another angle you can look from."

So, your job is to find that other angle, even if you don't believe it at the moment.

If you have a limiting belief about yourself, it helps to ask, "Is this really true?" Often, the answer is, "No, this belief is *not* true." You'll learn to tell yourself, "There's another angle here. Or there's another angle over there."

Whether you think that you're not good enough or that you're shy or that you're not worthy—you can always disprove that limiting belief.

And the way to disprove a limiting belief is to replace it with an empowering new belief and then take action based on this new belief.

For example, my parents, as Russian immigrants, gave me some limiting beliefs about my being Russian and *not* being good enough.

But I decided to look at it from another perspective, and I realized that there are many Russians who are intelligent, cultured, and sophisticated. I even started to believe that Russian girls are sexy, like the Bond girls in spy movies.

So, I chose to use these new empowering beliefs.

I realized that I wanted to let go of the limiting beliefs because they were *not* serving me.

So, what did I need to do? I needed to switch to the empowering beliefs that I learned from some positive people.

Even though in the beginning, I might have not believed the empowering beliefs, I resolved: *"I am going to do it, anyway."*

I learned to improve my inner dialogue. I spend a few minutes every day instilling a new, empowering belief in myself. I choose what I focus on with my mind.

Find something in yourself that you really love and appreciate and focus more on *that*.

Remember, confidence and assertiveness come with experience and with time. The more you put yourself out there in situations where you feel uncomfortable—but you do it, anyway—the more your confidence builds.

Continue practicing your mindfulness, awareness, meditation, and presence.

Natalie Glebova is an empowerment coach, author, and former Miss Universe. She has been intensely focused on women empowerment and gender equality activism for the last decade. As a He4She advocate, a campaign by UN Women, she is very passionate about encouraging young people to build their self-confidence and reach their biggest goals. She is currently teaching a course "Empowered YOU" at Bangkok University to international students about effective goal setting, mastering self-discipline, finding a purpose in life, and positive thinking.

A graduate of IT Management from Ryerson University in Toronto, Canada, she also has a certificate in Nutrition and Sport from Washington State University. Natalie has been actively involved in charity work ever since she moved to Thailand in 2006 and was a spokesperson for worldwide and local organizations including Habitat for Humanity and Operation Smile.

She has written two best-selling books: *Healthy Happy Beautiful* and *I AM WINNING—A Guide to Personal Empowerment.* Her public seminars and online empowerment training courses are centered around having the habits and the mindset that will make you a winner in life. https://natalieglebova.com

* * * * * *

Gamify Your Wealth
Principle #8
As you log each time you complete an important action, you build two things. You build evidence that you are putting in the work. You also build your confidence that you are getting better at your chosen task.

I often say, "Confidence is built on evidence." Logging each completed action can energize you. It can give you the power to keep going. That's truly helpful.

Here's a powerful benefit. Logging an accomplished action can give you a form of pleasure. How? You can enjoy a feeling of accomplishment. Better than that, you can create hope in your heart. You're making progress. You DO have hope in your life.

* * * * * *

Gamify Grid #8 (Example)	
Action	Keep a log of your purchases for two months. Compare your purchase choices. Are you being more careful with your purchase choices? Are you saving money?
Token	Place a button in a jar.
Date Start	2/01/20__
Date Completion	5/01/20__
Self-Reward	Get a neck massage from a massage therapist.

Now, it's your turn to fill out the Gamify Grid.

Gamify Grid	
Action	
Token	
Date Start	
Date Completion	
Self-Reward	

Important Point to Remember:
Shift from "How am I doing?" to "How are YOU doing?"

Power Questions:
When will you rehearse* with a friend? How will you practice shifting to "How are YOU doing?"

* You can go to GetTheBigYES.com/yes and connect with me about the possibility of my coaching you directly. I help clients with my unique Directed-Rehearsal™.

Chapter 10

Use the W.E.A.L.T.H. System Elevate Your Influence (Part 4)

She was way out of my league. Looked like a model. How could I capture her attention?

I saw a piano. I strode to it and played my original music.

She was intrigued. She sat down. She mentioned that she wrote poetry.

I gently asked, "Do you have a line that you'd like to share?"

She shared a line of her writing.

I wrote a melody.

She smiled.

I celebrated her words. Set them to music. Made her feel important. Cherished.

We had a relationship. For a time.

From that time forward, I always remember to **celebrate the other person. Make them feel important.**

"Make the other person feel important—and do it sincerely." – Dale Carnegie

What is the secret to true influence?

It is: Want something so much that **you'll do everything to learn how to make other people feel important.**

When you master connecting and making other people feel important, you gain real support.

People will want to be around you. They will want to see you succeed. (Not all people you meet, but enough.)

Where do we start?

You need to have magnetic energy. Throughout my life, I have attracted several people who became team members, colleagues, and friends. How? I radiate a hopeful, positive energy. Because I know what I want and every day I move forward.

I have purpose and joy. More than that…

I focus on:

I can be sunshine wherever I stand.

So, let's find out what you truly want.

I invited Marc Allen (author, president, and publisher of New World Library) to share with my readers his discoveries about *creating a life you truly love:*

Move Beyond Abundance to a Life of True Fulfillment by Marc Allen

The first step to discovering the secret of manifestation is to write your ideal scene on paper, your dream life five years in the future. Begin with the end in mind and keep it in mind. The day I turned thirty, I sat down and took a sheet of paper and wrote Ideal Scene at the top. I imagined everything had gone as well as I could possibly imagine and somehow, over the next five years, I was able to create the ideal life for me. What would it look like? What would I do and have, and who would I be?

I was surprised, even shocked in a strange way, at what came spilling out on paper. I imagined I had a publishing company, successfully publishing books and music, including my own books and music. Before I sat down and wrote out my ideal scene, I had absolutely no interest in business. I had never taken a business course. I had never written a book or recorded my music. The words that spilled out when I wrote my ideal scene surprised me as much as they were to surprise just about everyone else I knew.

I imagined I wrote successful books and recorded beautiful music as well. I imagined I had a lovely white house on a hill in northern California, one of my favorite places on earth. I imagined I had a wonderfully loving relationship. I dared to imagine my ideal, so I imagined I had plenty of time for it all: creativity, a successful business, friends and family, and plenty of time alone for myself as well … That was my ideal: success with ease, and success without compromising the other things that were important to me in life …

The second step to discovering the secret of manifestation is to write your goals as affirmations, beginning with "In an easy and relaxed manner, in a healthy and positive way … " Years later, looking back, I realized how powerful those words were—so powerful, in fact, that by repeating them daily, I overcame many of my doubts and fears …

The next step to discovering the secret of manifestation is

to write a one-page plan for every major goal …

The final step to discovering the secret of manifestation is to take action …

We know the secret, deep in our hearts. We've always known the secret. To love one another and all of creation, is the greatest secret of all. Love overcomes fear and transforms our lives and our world.

Marc Allen is a renowned author and president and publisher of New World Library, which he co-founded with Shakti Gawain in 1977. Guiding the company from a small start-up with no capital to its current position as one of the leading independent publishers in the country, Marc has shepherded some of the most influential non-fiction books of the past 30 years, including *The Power of Now* by Eckhart Tolle, *The Seven Spiritual Laws of Success* by Deepak Chopra, and *Creative Visualization* by Shakti Gawain.

Marc is the author of several life-changing books, including *Visionary Business, A Visionary Life, The Millionaire Course, The Greatest Secret of All,* the newly revised *Tantra for the West,* and his most recent publication *The Magical Path.*

As a gifted speaker and seminar leader, Marc works with people around the globe to craft lives of lasting abundance and prosperity. www.MarcAllen.com

* * * * * *

Gamify Your Wealth

Principle #9

When your Gamify Pattern grows stale, change something. Prepare for backsliding.

Here's an example. Stephanie sets up a morning pattern. She gets up early and goes for a run. Then she's working late, and she needs more sleep.

She starts missing her morning run. She feels bad.

Fortunately, Stephanie makes a shift. She changes her routine. She goes for a run immediately after work. Then, Stephanie has dinner and cools down.

If something does not work any longer, change it.

At one point, I was exercising after a day of work at a strenuous job. I would get certain back pains. Once in a while, I would postpone my weight training session for one day. I wanted to be careful about causing myself any injury.

The truth is: We all experience days when we cannot fulfill a planned action.

Prepare for backsliding. Create a plan so you are ready if you miss an exercise session. You have pre-selected how you fit in your next exercise session.

Avoid giving up. Certainly, avoid berating yourself. Just get up and step forward again.

It does not matter how slowly you go so long as you do not stop.
– Confucius

* * * * * *

Gamify Grid #9 (Example)	
Action	Exercise daily.
Token	Place a coin into a jar.
Date Start	9/3/20__
Date Completion	On-going. The first reward is in five days.
Self-Reward	First Self-Reward: something fun with a friend—a dinner (or something you prefer).

Now, it's your turn to fill out the Gamify Grid.

Gamify Grid	
Action	
Token	
Date Start	
Date Completion	
Self-Reward	

Important Point to Remember:
Prepare for backsliding. Keep moving forward.

Power Question:
If you backslide, how will you get up and keep moving forward?

Chapter 11

Use the W.E.A.L.T.H System Advantage (Part 1)

When I was nine years old, my eyes lit up, receiving a film camera from my father. He also gave me a film projector. My life leapt forward. Filmmaking! Wow. I was totally engaged. Energized to overcome my timid, shy, patterns. I was timid, playing piano for seniors. Intimidated. Apologizing for being alive.

But with a film camera in my hand, I was the visionary, the storyteller, the magician, the leader.

I had to learn to lead people, including leading my father, the non-active Marine. My first camera operator.

At ten years old, I won an award…okay an "honorable mention." But that was a start. Later, I earned a University Media Award and a special award at the Emmy Awards.

Years later, some young people approached me after I taught the Interactive Workshop *Ignite Your Sales Success: Avoid Big Mistakes that Cost You Sales* at Hacker Dojo in

Silicon Valley, California.

They asked about getting the attention of an investor.

One talked about the statistic of getting a 2% response rate to mass emailing.

I listened.

Then I asked, "Have you won an award or something?"

I emphasized that it's important to show you have skills and the ability to complete projects. You want to demonstrate that appropriate people have recognized your exceptional work. If possible.

Here's an important principle: **You must submit your work to gain any awards.**

Recently, I was looking through an old file. I saw that one of my films had been shown at the Philadelphia International Film Festival. I had not thought about that in years!

Here is an important point:

"No submission. No chance at a third-party endorsement."

You need to develop your advantage. Become an A.C.E.

The A.C.E. System

A – advantage for other person
C – capture attention on the world stage
E – engage the second sentence

1. Advantage for the other person.

Begin a message (conversation, text, voicemail) with an advantage for the other person. Researchers note that human beings tend to function on a survival level. They are always looking for an advantage and ways to survive. Capture people's curiosity and their attention by being straightforward about the advantage. You can say, "Here is an advantage so you can..."

2. **Capture attention on the world stage.**

Be sure to capture the other person's attention by noting a third-party endorsement.

It is skillful to express an endorsement in a way that seems like you're just telling a story.

Here's an example: "When I took the stage to accept an XY Award, I realized that..."

Soon after graduating college, I wrote, produced, and directed a feature film. How?

In the previous years, I had won a series of awards for short films and a music video. As I mentioned, I won a special award at the Emmy Awards. This recognition helped convince a co-producer, a California Motion Picture Commissioner, and investors to support me and my first feature film.

When I need someone to quickly know my qualifications, I can quietly mention some experience that shows I have accomplished certain milestones. Just a few milestones include: I have taught MBA students at Stanford University, Sofia University, and California State University—Chico. I have given workshops and speeches from New York to New Zealand—including Thailand and Silicon Valley, California.

Remember to submit your work for possible awards.

Carefully mention your accomplishments.

Also, remember, the person does not know you. **How can you get them to give you any time or consideration? Show that you have proof of your expertise.**

Here is a pattern you might adapt (for an email):

Here's an advantage for when you need to convince an investor to fund your project. When I stepped onto the stage to accept an XY Award, I realized…

3. Engage the second sentence.

The first sentence is the advantage for the other person. The second sentence is the one that you alert the person that you have a third-party endorsement.

I learned this idea from Guy Kawasaki: "If you don't toot your own horn, don't complain that there's no music."

It's important that people know that you are credible. You also want them to know you complete projects. You're trustworthy.

However, I suggest that you go back to talking about the advantage after the second sentence.

Why?

People often dislike someone who comes across as too self-centered.

A classic story is:

A self-centered actor droned on about his accomplishments. Then, he said, "That's enough about me. So how did you like my movie?"

Again, I emphasize that you make the sentence sound like you're telling a story.

Here's an example of a second sentence plus additional sentences.

I learned so much while directing my first feature film. I learned a) Guard Momentum and b) Protect the Talent.

What are you concerned about?

If you could effectively lead a team, would that turn things around?

You notice that I return to the reader's concerns.

"You can make more friends in two months by becoming interested in other people than you can in two years by trying to get other people interested in you." – Dale Carnegie

* * * * * *

I interviewed Henry Wong, a venture capitalist and successful entrepreneur. He reveals the essentials of making a great pitch.

Interview with Henry Wong

Tom: When somebody makes a pitch what is crucial for them to do?

Henry: The pitch has to be clear, precise, and self-explanatory in 25 words. Sometimes, at a cocktail party, you walk up to somebody who may be the CEO or a major partner of a venture capital firm. You say, "I have this project."

The CEO says, "What do you got?"

You have 60 seconds for your spiel, and you have to exactly describe what you do. Clear, precise, and crisp.

Tom: What is the big mistake that somebody, who is delivering a pitch, must avoid?

Henry: They don't know what they want. They don't know what they have discovered. They are just not sure about themselves. When one is not sure of oneself, it shows in the language and the delivery of the verbal communication. If you don't know what the hell you're doing, I don't want to fund you. You're kidding me, right?

Tom: Knowing what you know now, what would you have done differently in business?

Henry: I would have been like a machine. If a guy does not fit the department, I would have fired him. Learn how to fire people. Not as bad as Steve Jobs. But learn how to cut the cancer cells away from your company. For example, I was the manager of a bullpen of nine people. They were different types of telemarketers who handled the sales of software.

One guy in the bullpen was so negative. Instead of taking phone calls and making phone calls, he would just walk around and talk to the other people. He was negative—complain, complain, complain. As a manager, I was a good guy. I gave him a verbal warning and two written warnings. I asked, "Do you want to work at this company?" And I didn't fire him. I was so nice. I followed procedure, but sometimes you cannot let the procedure run you. You have to fire the bad apple. It's like the old phrase: One bad apple will spoil the bunch."

Professor Henry H. Wong has been a prolific and successful venture investor, serial entrepreneur, and Stanford University Mentor in Silicon Valley during the last 43 years.

After working for four Fortune 100 corporations, Henry channeled his entrepreneurial spirit to go and "change the world."

Frustrated with existing sloppy edge technologies, Henry founded, seed-funded, and exited five successful startups, including SS8 Networks (ADC Telecom), IP Communications (Nokia), XaQti Semiconductor (Vitesse), CNet Technology (IPO), and Combinet (Cisco). He was always the founder, chairman, first president, and CEO.

Professor Henry has successful experience in selling his startup Combinet to Cisco for US$165M in 1995 money valuation.

Realizing that "money makes the world go round," Henry founded Diamond TechVentures, a Transpacific Venture Investment firm. In parallel, he was also the venture partner to Guy Kawasaki's Garage Technology Ventures, and before that, Crystal Ventures, a Taiwan President Lee's $250M VC Fund.

With the fast growth in Silicon Valley and the ever-changing landscape of technological advancement, a different ecosystem is needed to accommodate growth and accelerate prosperity. To address this, Henry founded TechLAB, an Innovation Center, where he coined the term, "Find it, Fix it & Fund it." Pre-qualified startups or companies that Henry continues to help are incubated inside this accelerator under a secured environment, where the filing of new patentable technologies is done on-site.

The Singapore government's SPRING agency funded Henry's iStartUP program to train Singapore entrepreneurs. The Hong Kong government honored Henry as the "Game Changer" returnees with the Home Coming Tipping Point award. The IT Minister Choi Yanghee of the Korean government recognizes Henry's continuous contribution to their Knowledge Innovation Center (KIC) and named him an Advisor to South Korea.

Henry holds a Business degree from the University of Utah and an MBA in Telecom Management from Golden Gate University. He is an MBA Professor at Sofia University and is a Mentor at Stanford University. He was a 2002 finalist for the Ernst & Young "Entrepreneur of the Year Award." Henry is a frequent Keynote Speaker, Panel Discussion contributor, and a Business Plan Competition

Judge.

See a Video on Professor Henry Wong's Stanford University Lecture: https://bit.ly/2MJhqCT

Professor Henry H. Wong is available as a Keynote Speaker, Business Plan Competition Judge, or member of a Panel.

Subject to availability, Professor Wong can provide in-house training on "From Garage to IPO" customized for Incubators, accelerators, science parks, corporate strategic planning departments, and government agencies. For further details, please email HenryWong94301@Yahoo.com

* * * * * *

(We usually have a Principle here. I will reveal Principle #10 in a later section.)

* * * * * *

Gamify Grid #10 (Example)	
Action	Reduce eating too much sugar.
Token	Place a coin in a jar.
Date Start	6/2/20__
Date Completion	Ongoing. First Self-Reward 20 days later. 6/22/20__
Self-Reward	Purchase a new video game

Now, it's your turn to fill out the Gamify Grid…

Gamify Grid	
Action	
Token	
Date Start	
Date Completion	
Self-Reward	

Important Point to Remember:
Submit your work so you can possibly earn an award.

Power Question:
How can you gain recognition to prove that you are effective and credible?

Chapter 12

Use the W.E.A.L.T.H System Advantage (Part 2)

George Takei, (who portrayed Mr. Sulu of *Star Trek,* the original TV series), invited me to take a chair.

We were meeting to discuss a possible role for him in my first feature film.

I was in my 20s and stunned to have gained an audience with him.

I showed him my storyboards.

The scene featured the lead character, an Asian man, sitting at his desk. Worried. 3 AM. The world for him is shattering. A lone tear slides down his face and lands in a teacup. Causing a tsunami to rise in the teacup.

In slow motion.

Kindly, George said, "Uhhh. Tom. Isn't that a bit melodramatic?"

I learned two things from George.

First, how to deliver coaching in a kind, warm manner.

Two, how to throw out storyboards and avoid filming a scene that I would drop from the film, anyway.

I had storyboarded that scene because I had come from the world of producing and directing music videos. If I had set the melodramatic scene to a pop song, it could have worked—in a music video.

George's guidance and friendliness are parts of what makes him a "Category of One."

To have a real advantage, develop yourself and what you offer to the marketplace as a Category of One. By this I mean, you hold a whole category to yourself. That is, no one provides what you offer.

Here is the **Category of One System**

O – offer is unique
N – no competition
E – engage scarcity

1. Offer is unique.

You want to enter the marketplace as a Category of One. That means your offer is unique. There's no other solution like it. Then, people need to go to you for your unique solution offering unique benefits.

Here is an example:
Tom Marcoux – Category of One

- Code Access Reset™
- Directed-Rehearsal™
- Hidden Breakthrough Session
- Your Personalized Secret Strategy Report
- Gamify Your Wealth System

When I talk about gamify, I say:

Gamify or fail to fly.
Set the score and get some more.

I have developed my own systems of coaching and empowering clients, students, and audiences.

I also say,
I'm the Communication Sage
'Cause I lean into my age.
Don't come to me for theories.
I got wisdom for your queries.

I help people create more time, less stress, and zero procrastination.

They elevate their personal energy. How?

They develop something I call Action-Hope.

In another section of this book, I talk about how Hope has a F.O.R.M.

F – freedom
O – opportunity
R – realize fulfillment
M – meaning

What about you? How can you develop your skills and bring something uniquely beneficial to the marketplace?

2. No competition.

Imagine the power of offering something unique. That elevates what you're doing. Then, you have no competition. You don't have to devote resources or time to trying to distinguish yourself from other vendors or suppliers in a particular category.

Instead, you offer a product or service that is a Category of One.

Unfortunately, many of us enter an already glutted field where the competitors have already established a stranglehold on the marketplace. Don't play that game. Create a new game. Then, you will have no competition.

3. Engage scarcity.

When you are the only one offering a unique product or service, it's natural that scarcity is involved. There are limits. You can only serve so many customers.

So, this becomes an advantage. Why? People often want what they can't have. The old phrase *available while supplies last* pushes people to take action. Using scarcity is often a tactic that works.

* * * * * *

(We usually have a Principle here. I will reveal
The final principle—Principle #10—in a later section.)

* * * * * *

Gamify Grid #11 (Example)	
Action	Record your podcast episode
Token	Place a coin in a jar
Date Start	11/1/20__
Date Completion	11/8/20__
Self-Reward	Give yourself two real days off. No checking email. No chores around the house.

Now, it's your turn to fill out the Gamify Grid…

Gamify Grid	
Action	
Token	
Date Start	
Date Completion	
Self-Reward	

Important Point to Remember:

Develop an advantage when you make your offer a Category of One.

Power Question:

What can you offer that truly serves buyers? How can you release them from enduring a burning pain point?

Chapter 13

Use the W.E.A.L.T.H System Advantage (Part 3)

"I'm so proud of you!" said the younger woman after the shy, timid woman gave a speech in my Public Speaking college course.

This experience turned around my thoughts about the phrase "proud of you."

Witnessing the young woman support her friend so powerfully, I realized something new…

To say "I'm proud of you" means

- I celebrate who you are
- You matter
- Your courage, persistence, and commitment all matter.
- I appreciate you and your efforts
- You are a worthwhile person
- I see you
- Your destiny matters

On hearing me tell this story, my friend Aaron Parnell, known as the Posture Genius*, said that "I'm proud of you" is about…

*"You are on the right track to becoming the best person God made you to be." – Aaron Parnell**

*See Repostu0ringInstituteofAmerica.org

The journey of creating true, sustainable wealth can feel exhausting. It helps to add to your daily path the process of targeting a Big Payday.

Target the Big Payday

Use the B.I.G. System

B – build alliances
I – increase your influence with special skills
G – gain leverage

1. Build alliances.

If you buy property, and you hire a property manager, you have formed an alliance. Otherwise, if you buy a property and you manage it yourself…you bought a job.

I write screenplays with a writing partner. That's one of the best alliances of my life.

I say, "We're stronger together."

Our alliance began when a friend of mine said, "There's a screenwriting contest being run by a division of Director Ron Howard's company."

I thought I would pass the opportunity on to one of my

former college students.

He replied, "I will enter that screenwriting contest—with you co-writing the screenplay with me, Tom."

I said that I would think about it.

I thought this would be a tough decision. One that would take a lot of time.

It all came down to one question: "Do I trust him?"

I called him back and I said, "I'm in."

Writing screenplays, especially ones in certain genres, can lead to potential Big Paydays.

What alliances do you need to make?

2. Increase your influence with special skills.

My writing partner and I write screenplays. Selling a screenplay can lead to a big payday.

Sometimes, multiple companies bid on a screenplay. That's when a screenplay may gain a million-dollar fee or more.

Over the years, my writing partner and I have elevated and honed our screenwriting skills.

As I mentioned, we began by entering a screenwriting contest. But there was too little time to develop a finely honed screenplay. We did not win. But we kept going with further drafts of the screenplay.

Our skills are so much improved over where we began—in our collaborative efforts.

You need to develop skills that are in demand.

It's important to remember,

People pay more for what is less available.
That is, people pay more for special skills.

For example, more people have skills to work at fast food restaurants, and journalists report that fast food restaurants pay "poverty wages."

When I say, "increase your influence with special skills" I mean connect to something you truly want to devote time and effort to.

Plenty of people have the skills to work at a McDonald's.

However, few people are screenwriters. Even fewer are good screenwriters. That takes time, effort, study, many drafts of projects, and more.

Who is willing to hone their skills and put in the required effort?

The high-level skills can make you valuable to the marketplace. Keep your eyes wide open. The marketplace changes all the time.

3. Gain leverage

When one person works for an hour, that effort yields limited value. On the other hand, when one person leads a team of 10 people, then the value is multiplied.

When working with team members, I say, "We're stronger together."

Look at how you can do work one time, and it provides financial compensation year after year. I have books, eBooks, and online courses that bring in income year after year.

How can you gain leverage?

What can you try on a small scale—so, you learn and discover good possibilities?

* * * * * *

(I will reveal Principle #10—in a later section.)

Gamify Grid #12 (Example)	
Action	Begin the path of expanding your skills. Use Google, study possibilities, and take a course. Read books, blogs and more.
Token	Use a jellybean and place it into a cardboard box.
Date Start	3/3/20__
Date Completion	Ongoing. The first reward is in seven days.
Self-Reward	Pick a hobby and purchase something that helps you move forward. (For example, get yarn for knitting.)

Now, it's your turn to fill out the Gamify Grid…

Gamify Grid	
Action	
Token	
Date Start	
Date Completion	
Self-Reward	

Important Point to Remember:

It's valuable to devote thinking and effort to develop a Big Payday.

Power Question:

What are you going to do this week to expand your personal leverage?

Chapter 14

Use the W.E.A.L.T.H System
Listen

"Your dreams mean nothing," one of my relatives said. He was talking about a nightmare that I had shared with him.

Unfortunately, he missed an opportunity to simply listen to me.

Over many years, this guy would not ask me a question.

All he did was push his opinions.

I saw him drop friends.

He became a "reverse example" to me. I looked at his results and thought, "I want something different for my life. I'll learn to listen to people and develop healthy connections."

I learned that it's smart to do two things: Ask questions and demonstrate that I care about what another person is going through. It's also a more joyful way of living.

I share with my clients and audiences:

When you're listening, you're winning.

Show that You're Truly Listening with Select Nonverbal Behaviors

Use the N.O.D. system.

N – nod
O – open and smile
D – direct your attention to them

1. Nod.

One of my mentors taught me a vital detail. When you are listening to someone, be sure to nod. In the American culture, that is moving your chin up and down.

Some people hesitate to nod because they think that it means that they're saying, "Yes, I agree with what you're saying."

However, a nod can mean, "I'm listening. Okay. You have that opinion." Nodding in this situation is a way of showing that you're paying attention. You are demonstrating respect for the person.

2. Open and smile.

My nonverbal technique of "open" is about turning completely toward the person. I call this "heart faces heart."

I call this technique "open" because the opposite is to cross your arms and to hold yourself back.

You are signaling with your crossed arms that you are *closed* to letting something in. This is an interpretation that many people believe.

The truth is: Some people cross their arms because they're cold. Or they might feel more comfortable with their arms crossed. Several female individuals find comfort in crossing their arms.

However, in several cultures, people are taught that crossed arms mean closed off. So, you want to open. Open the conversation to a positive connection.

Also, remember to smile. There are a couple of important details related to smiling. One, let the smile naturally come up on your face and naturally fall off your face. Some people keep the smile on too long; it looks phony. It causes more trouble. People who are leaders who are confident in their ability to make a situation better, naturally smile at some points and naturally release the smile.

At one point, I was looking at different corporations and looking at the videos of the CEOs and presidents. What happened to these people? How did it happen that they forgot how to smile? Are they just trying to show that they're tough in these videos? That they're serious? They have no warmth. Is it that they don't care about anyone?

Instead, realize the power of a warm smile.

3. Direct your attention to them.

When the other person talks, direct your attention to the person. By this I mean, have all your nonverbal behaviors say, *"I'm right here. You're the most important person in this room to me. I am not looking over your shoulder for someone richer so that I can drop you like a hot potato and go talk to the rich person. My attention is on you. You are important. I care about what you care about. I'm listening to you because you deserve my full attention and respect."*

How do you do this? You face them. Heart faces heart.

You smile when appropriate. They say something painful. You pause. You feel the pain. It shows on your face. Your tone reflects that it bothers you, too. You might even say, "I'm sorry to hear that."

One big thing I learned is when to say, "I'm sorry." I had mentors who said, "Don't say I'm sorry unless you broke it."

But then I learned that saying "I'm sorry" when appropriate is a fast way to communicate: "I'm concerned. I'm sad that something hurts you. It is important to me that you were hurt, and you're letting me know about it. I am here now. Paying attention to you and your pain. You are important. Your feelings are important."

* * * * * *

Gain Mentors. Identify People to Listen To.

Mentors can catapult your wealth journey forward. Gain mentors. More than one.

You can listen well.

You do not have to follow their advice. But sometimes, you develop a great relationship. I have learned:

Gain a mentor. They can open doors that you cannot at this point.

Here, Bob Burg, Hall of Fame Speaker and co-author of the best-selling *Go-Giver* series of books, shares crucial insights.

Interview with Bob Burg

(lightly edited)

Tom: Bob, I would love to hear: What is the essence of the *Go-Giver* series (of books) and philosophy?

Bob: It really comes down to understanding that shifting your focus is really the key. Shifting your focus from getting to giving.

When we say giving in this context, we simply mean constantly and consistently providing immense value to others. And that doing so is not only a nice way, a pleasant way of conducting business, but the most financially profitable way as well.

Tom: Got it. We've noticed in your material you talked about mentorship. **What should a person avoid doing when they're trying to get a mentor?**

Bob: Mentorship is so important. And it's so helpful. It can really cut one's learning curve by years. Yet what I find a lot of people do is when they approach someone to mentor them, they'll come out and this is someone with whom they don't have a relationship, they'll just say, "Hey, would you be my mentor?"

It's sort of like asking, "Hey, would you share 40 years of your experience with me even though you don't know me from a hole in the wall."

Johanna (co-host): Wow.

Bob: Yeah, and I think it can come across as entitled in a way and maybe not respectful of the process. While there might be some people who might say yes, it's pretty doubtful.

But what you can do is instead ask someone, whether it's online or it's in person, you can certainly frame it in such a way as to say, "I really admire your work. If this is not appropriate or just not something you'd like to do, it's totally understandable, but may I ask you one or two very specific questions?" When you do that, you've done a few things. One, you respected the process. You've come across not as though you're entitled to their wisdom, but that you realize it's a big ask.

And, two, you're giving them the out or backdoor. You're letting them know, "Hey if this is not appropriate or just not something you want to do—totally understandable. I know you're very busy."

Also, by saying "one or two very specific questions," you're letting them know that they're not going to waste their time.

It's not like you're asking, "Can I pick your brain?" Instead, "I've got one or two," and that says to the person, "This is a person who means business. This is a person who isn't going to waste my time. This is the person who just wants some good advice."

Most likely, they'll be willing to share that with you. Not always. But it doesn't have to be always. It doesn't have to be everyone, but many people will. Now, you want to make sure that you research that person and don't ask anything that you could have known the answer to through research because that will be kind of counterproductive.

Also, after the conversation, after you thank them, I would, as soon as you leave, write, and send a handwritten personalized thank-you note. Just something such as, "Thank you so much again for taking time out of your day. I understand you're very busy. Please know how grateful I am. I look forward to applying the wisdom you shared and will let you know how things are progressing.'

Then, what I'd also do, and this is just a really nice touch (and again, you've researched them, so you know their favorite charity), is make a small—doesn't have to be anything big, but just a small—donation in their name to their favorite charity or cause. It'll get back to them; they'll be notified. You're not doing it to kiss up to them, but again, just to show, to communicate that you're respecting the process and that you want to, in some way, be of value to them.

Now, you can always come back three weeks later or a month later, follow up, maybe ask another question. And if, over time, a mentor-protege relationship is supposed to develop, it will. If not, it won't. You might find that there are different people who are one-time or two-time mentors. You might really hit it off with that one person, and they take an interest in you. But remember a mentor-protege relationship is a relationship, and it builds over time.

Tom: Excellent. Right now, I'm working on my 54th book [This book you are reading.]

Bob: 54th!

Tom: I am curious as to how you'll respond to a specific question. **What has been a Miracle-Secret—that is, something that has created profound good in your life?**

Bob: I think it's two parts of one whole. In the first part, there is very much an interest in others and a desire to help people feel genuinely good about themselves. This is something I think I've really gotten from my parents. I think that to the degree that you are truly interested in another person, that's really the degree they feel good about you. So, it comes back, and it provides you with a really unique advantage in life. Because you've got more people who are on your side. You've got more people who know you, who like you, who trust you.

And I think while the interest in others wasn't necessarily

natural for me, I think I got that from really modeling my folks. What was natural to me was a very strong sense of empathy. I'm able to really kind of feel other people's pain and on a deep level understand the emotions they're feeling. And because of that, I think that leads again to people trusting me more naturally and quicker than they may otherwise. I see powerful, laser-focus stuff.

Be able to move from an 'I' focus or 'me' focus to what we call an 'other' focus. And that is really looking to laser focus, if you will, on how you can bring or provide or give value to others. When we do that, we really create the context for a relationship with that person. So, you focus on the other person. There's nothing self-sacrificial or martyr-ish about it. It's just a pleasant way of living life and conducting business.

As we mentioned earlier, it happens to be the most effective way to be profitable, financially but also profitable in terms of social relationships or family relationships or whatever it may be. To the degree that we look to provide value to our world, to other people, to the marketplace, that's the degree that it naturally comes back to us.

Johanna (co-host): Great point. **Knowing what you know now, what would you have done differently?**

Bob: I love that question because it really allows us to reflect back and reflect back on our mistakes, which I've made plenty of and continue to, but hopefully at a slower pace than when I was younger.

I think one of the reasons why is because when I was younger, I pretty much thought I had it figured out. I really felt as though I understood the way the world worked. I felt I understood human nature, and really felt I knew the answers.

It reminds me of a quote that is often attributed to Mark

Twain, although he's not recorded as ever saying it. But then again, anything that's really clever or wise, we figure either Mark Twain or Ben Franklin or, somebody like that said it. But the quote is, 'It ain't what you don't know that gets you into trouble; it's what you're absolutely positively sure you do know that just ain't so.'

Tom: Yes.

Bob: And that was me. I just knew that I knew these things, but really, I didn't. And it was only as I began to get a little older and started to mature in that way and begin listening more and talking less that the mistakes didn't come as quickly and as furiously.

Tom: Understood. We have a situation where we have a salesperson, and they have allowed their enthusiasm to be too big and too much, and the person says, 'Whoa, hey, you're pushing.' What would you invite that salesperson to do when they find that they're in a situation where someone's giving them a lot of resistance?

Bob: And it happens to be very true that enthusiasm, as good as it is, can, when you go overboard in your enthusiasm, you will actually turn people off. You'll create the offensive, nauseating thing. You'll actually have them put up mental blocks and sometimes verbal locks, such as 'back off.' Maybe not exactly like that, but that's really what it is.

So, the first thing is to learn a lesson from it and understand that we have to temper our enthusiasm so that we don't come across in a way that is overdone.

But I would say the first thing to do is to apologize.

Johanna (co-host): Yes.

Bob: You say, 'My apologies. I tend to be so enthusiastic about this because of my personal understanding of it. But really, you know, that's not the correct way to be. My job is to really find out what your needs are and see if this product or service will meet those needs.'

Tom: Got it. What if a person is trying to sell something or offer something, but the person is being extremely defensive about it?

Bob: That can certainly happen. So, let's say you never met this person before. You're sitting down with them about to do a presentation, and they kind of let you know up front, 'Hey, don't think I'm buying anything today,' or, 'Don't think I'm some easy sale or some easy mark.'

And remember, we don't know what's in another person's head and what's in another person's heart. As human beings, we all see the world in our own way based on our own experiences. Maybe she's saying she's not an easy mark because she really does believe she is, and so is a little bit trying to set a boundary.

Or maybe, she was taken advantage of. Who knows why? So, whatever the case is, she has kind of set an adversarial type of frame. And if we, as the sales professional, if we buy into that, then we're defensive. And we're kind of trying to let her know, 'Hey, I'm just trying.'

And nothing good is going to come out of that. You're just going to have two people basically against each other. No one's going to win because she's not going to buy, and you're not going to sell.

So, let's instead reset the frame. A frame is simply the foundation from which everything else takes place. So obviously, that's not a frame we want to operate within.

We'll reset the frame. Instead, we wait after she says that. We pause for a moment. We certainly don't argue.

We simply say, 'You know, Mary, while we've been able to help a lot of people with this product, whether or not it's the right solution for you, we simply can't know without exploring deeper and discovering whether it meets your needs. So please know this conversation is for both of us to determine that. And if it does, great. If not, that's okay too.'

Tom: Excellent.

Bob: Yeah. We've now reset that from one of two adversaries to one of two allies who are looking for the same thing: what's in her best interest."

Tom: This reminds me of one of your books that I read called *Adversaries into Allies.*

Bob: That's right. Terrific.

Tom: I've also read your book, *Endless Referrals*. I've also read a couple of your books in your *Go-Giver* series. Particularly, I remember the title *Go-Givers Sell More*.

Bob: Yeah. Thank you. I appreciate that.

Tom: Right and I know your most recent book is called *Go-Giver Influencer.*

Bob. Yes.

Tom: I believe your co-author is John David Mann.

Bob: Yeah. He is a fantastic writer and storyteller.

Tom: Right. So, perhaps you and John together went, 'Ah, this is so great. I'm so glad that we're putting this one in this book.'

Bob: As we brought the story together and we looked at it from different points, we began with mastering your emotions because that's really where it all begins. If you can't do that; you're not even in the game. You need to be able to step into the other person's shoes. We understand that is very difficult to do. Since, we all see the world in a different way. So, the only way to do that is to really ask questions and then listen.

Maybe the last part, where we talk about letting go of having to be right—that might be what really brings it together. Letting go of having to be right doesn't mean you don't want to be right, of course, you do; we all do, we're human beings. Why wouldn't we want to be right? But what it does mean is that we keep our minds open to understanding the other person's point of view. We open up to the idea that we may not be 100 percent right. There may be things we don't know.

This is really the great part: Two things happen when you let go of having to be right. When you let go of your attachment to having to be right, one thing is you go into learning mode. You're able to learn.

Johanna (co-host): Good point!

Bob: Because there are some people, we usually see them online, and it is about: 'You know, my mind's made up; don't confuse me with the facts.'

Tom: Wow.

Bob: You can't learn that way. So, when you open up to not having to be right, you can learn. This empowers you and actually gives you more information and ups the odds that you will be right.

The second thing it does is just as important. When you let go of having to be right, you see a change in the other person. They come to understand that you're simply looking for the truth.

You're not looking to be right at all costs. You're not looking to be right by making them wrong. You simply want the truth. And when you do that, this person is much more likely to be open to dropping their defensiveness and perhaps moving to your side of the issue.

But until this person feels safe with us, until they feel comfortable with us, until they have some trust in us, they'll never allow themselves to move off their position.

Tom: Got it. Bob, that was terrific. In fact, it's interesting in one of our previous podcasts Johanna and I were talking about how **I have this phrase: *"I like to hold to perceptions more than opinions."*** *Because if I have a perception, I could just change it easily and quickly. Because I can take in some new data. There's some new evidence. But if I have an opinion, I might stand there and defend it. That might slow us down.*

So, that's an idea that I've been working with. I love words. That's why I'm the Spoken Word Strategist. I write every day. I feel that when we have some precision with our words like *perception not opinion*—we're able to take the conversation to a higher level. I really feel that, Bob, you've been sharing how to have all our interactions at a warmer, higher level. I want to thank you for sharing all that with us.

Bob: That means a lot to me. Thank you so much.

Tom: Bob, I'm curious. What is the process of you and John David Mann working together on a book?

Bob: It's really easy because John is an extraordinary writer and storyteller. I'm a how-to guy. It's not as though it's a matter of which of us writes better and that we have to go through it and determine John's a great writer. So, really, it's just such a joy and a pleasure. He takes ideas and just makes them so much better. Plus, he's, in his own right a very successful entrepreneur and great thinker. **Like you [Tom], he's a wordsmith.**

Tom: Thank you.

Bob: So, it's really just such a pleasure to have the honor of working with John.

Tom: Terrific. So, Johanna, I'm curious what are you going to keep from this conversation?

Johanna (co-host): Well, I really enjoyed the framing idea and also I really enjoyed letting go of not having to be right.

Tom: Excellent. I'll keep from this conversation the idea of being a go-giver is actually connected to us operating on a higher level, a warmer level, a level of connection that is something that makes things better for everyone involved. Is there something you'd like to add to that, Bob?

Bob: I think you both made fantastic points. It's really been a pleasure speaking with both of you. Getting to exchange ideas, that's really what it's all about.

Tom: Yes, fantastic. Bob, thank you so much for this conversation. We are really grateful that you shared with our listeners* all your insights. [*Succeed Even If Podcast]

Bob Burg shares how a subtle shift in focus is not only a more uplifting and fulfilling way of conducting business but the most financially profitable way, as well. For 30 years he's helped companies, sales leaders, and their teams to more effectively communicate their value, sell at higher prices with less resistance, and grow their businesses based on Endless Referrals.

Bob has regularly addressed audiences ranging in size from 50 to 16,000—sharing the platform with notables including today's top thought leaders, broadcast personalities, Olympic athletes and political leaders, including a former United States President.

Although for years he was best known for his book *Endless Referrals,* it's his business parable, *The Go-Giver* (coauthored with John David Mann) that captured the imagination of his readers.

The Go-Giver, a Wall Street Journal and BusinessWeek Bestseller, has sold over a million copies. Since its release, it has consistently stayed in the Top 25 on Porchlight's (formerly 800-CEO-READ Business Book Bestsellers List). The book has been translated into 30 languages. It was rated #10 on Inc. Magazine's list of the Most Motivational Books Ever Written, and it was on HubSpot's 20 Most Highly Rated Sales Books of All Time.

Bob is the author of a number of books on sales, marketing, and influence, with total book sales approaching two million copies.

The American Management Association named Bob one of the 30 Most Influential Leaders and he was named one of the Top 200 Most Influential Authors in the World by Richtopia.

Bob is an advocate, supporter, and defender of the Free Enterprise system, believing that the amount of money one makes is directly proportional to how many people they serve.

He is also an unapologetic animal fanatic and served on the Board of Directors of Furry Friends Adoption and Clinic in his town of Jupiter, Florida. See Burg.com

* * * * * *

Gamify Grid #11 (Example)	
Action	Pick a daily disciple. Perhaps, reading for 15 minutes—or exercise.
Token	Place a jellybean in a jar.
Date Start	1/1/20__
Date Completion	On-going.
Self-Reward	Every two weeks, give yourself four hours completely free from any chores or duties.

Now, it's your turn to fill out the Gamify Grid.

Gamify Grid	
Action	
Token	
Date Start	
Date Completion	
Self-Reward	

Important Point to Remember:

Gain a mentor. The person can open doors that you cannot at this point.

Power Question:

When will you rehearse important nonverbal techniques?

Chapter 15

Use the W.E.A.L.T.H System Timing and Planning (Part 1)

At one point, I was working in a retail organization.

One customer arrived already upset. Their tone and word choice demonstrated that they were trouble. They were in the mode of "I want to fight with someone."

When it was appropriate, I said, "I agree with you. That would be the logical thing to happen. I didn't make this system. I just live in it."

This worked. It helped the person calm down. It was a matter of tone. Also, it used the timing of words and rhythm.

Here is a classic quote:

"People will do anything for those who encourage their dreams, justify their failures, allay their fears, confirm their suspicions, and help them throw rocks at their enemies."

— Blair Warren

This quote is intense.

At this moment, we'll just look at "confirm their suspicions."

If you can authentically say, "I agree" to something the person says, you are building a connection.

As you expand your wealth, you may be working with the public. The more people you encounter, it is likely that you will meet toxic people.

To deal effectively with toxic people you need timing and techniques…

Handle Toxic People with the Power of "3 No's"

Who is draining your energy? Some toxic person, yes?

They can be a family member, your life partner (temporarily, yes?), or a stranger.

The problem with many of the books about handling toxic people is that they address the situation as if the toxic person is being rational.

Does that seem likely to you?

Here are the techniques I call the "3 No's."

- No resistance
- No contact
- No hesitation to direct their brain

1. No resistance.

What do you get when you argue with an unreasonable person? Nothing good. Instead, if the situation is not extreme, see if you can avoid resisting. My clients hear my comment: "There's nothing to teach."

Did the person come to you for advice? Unlikely.

How does the "No resistance" technique sound?

• I agree. It is a bad pattern. This store's leadership has this policy. Is there another way I can help you?

• Right. This does not make logical sense. Here's what I can do that might help you…

2. No contact.

If there is danger or abuse involved in the situation, the answer is no contact with the other person. For example, if there is an abusive, elderly relative on the phone, one can say:

• You're being mean. I need to leave this phone conversation. I am going. Good night. (One ends the phone call.)

If the other person may be violent toward you, get out and get to safety.

My mentor who taught me self-defense techniques (he also taught S.W.A.T. officers) said to me, "The best defense is not to be there."

4. No hesitation to direct their brain.

At one point, I was a manager in a retail organization. A customer came in irrational and furious. They said, "There is going to be a lawsuit. For three days, this company has done ___ and ____ wrong! I want your name, his name, and her name."

During the conversation, I said, "Sir, what can I do to help you *now*? What is it that you would like to see happen *now*?" I also said, "I am helping you *now*."

I directed the angry person by using the word "now." I had no hesitation in directing his brain to *now*. Ultimately, I de-escalated the person and the situation. Then, he apologized to me.

There are several methods to handle toxic people. These techniques shared here help in certain situations.

Think of adding these methods to your "toolkit" for dealing with tough situations.

One of my friends had to work for a middle manager. Someone known as "a jerk."

But one day, my friend walked into the office and saw the stressed-out look on the middle manager's face.

My friend said, "I just realized. You have a super-tough job."

The guy's face lit up. He said, "Finally, somebody gets it."

Imagine listening to people. Then, they feel that you are different. They look at you and think: "Finally, somebody gets it."

Many of us wish that toxic people would "just go away." We can pause and reframe our first thought.

"Grace has the final word." – Alan Cohen

By this, he means that *we can use everything stress, sadness, and separation as steppingstones as we learn to get stronger.*

When you get stronger, you can act with grace.

You can learn to take a breath and maintain your calm.

That's when you can be a trustworthy leader. To yourself and others.

"[If] you have passed through life without an opponent—no one can ever know what you are capable of, not even you." - Seneca

"When you have a principled mindset, it doesn't matter how rough or unclear the path is. In the end, it will always lead you to the destination that your moral compass has set." – Terence Gordon, filmmaker/aviator

It means a lot to me that when I asked Terence Gordon for a quote for this book, he shared the above comment. As film producers and film directors, both Terence and I share the rough battles of getting films and projects made. So many disappointments and setbacks. So many opponents. And we both never give up.

You can stay strong.

This book is designed to help you deal with opponents (in various forms). Then you reliably take action to create wealth and elevate your influence.

Build People's Trust with Your Timing and Responses

Jay Conrad Levinson, the bestselling author known as the Father of Guerilla Marketing, taught me several things about marketing. It was great to talk with him. Years ago, for a particular book, I and my co-author contacted Jay. He responded with his contribution.

Instantly
by Jay Conrad Levinson

I make tough situations better by eliminating them ASAP each time. One of life's greatest satisfactions for me seems to be throwing things away. Although you'd never know it to look around my home, I seem to be dedicated to removing stuff from my files, computer desktop, real desktop, in-basket, and to-do list. At the end of every workday, which means Monday through Wednesday to me, I delight in crossing the final task off the list in my datebook.

At the end of every year, I cross the line into true ecstasy when I fill several full-sized garbage cans with paper no longer needed. I feel pretty much the same when I relieve my hard drive of data nobody on earth will ever need again. I've learned that by dealing with work assignments only one time, I am able to gain a lot more precious free time for myself.

Instead of putting the work aside for a later date, I deal with it at the moment it comes in, so that I won't have to be involved with it ever again. People say that I'm a good e-mail correspondent. I answer that it's mainly because I don't like having e-mail to answer. That's why I'm getting back to you instantly.

Jay Conrad Levinson was the author of the bestselling marketing series in history, *Guerrilla Marketing,* plus 56 other business books. His books have sold over 21 million copies worldwide. And his guerrilla concepts have influenced marketing so much that his books appear in 43 languages and are required reading in MBA programs worldwide.

"Knowing that I'm going to die gives urgency and meaning to everything I do." – Neil deGrasse Tyson

When I talk about timing, I'm also looking at the timing in our thinking.

Many of us have certain negative thoughts that bombard us. Unless one meditates, perhaps, like a monk, these thoughts just show up.

Your choice is in the 2nd Thought—the Empowering 2nd Thought.

You can condition your Empowering 2nd Thought. How? You choose empowering-thoughts and practice them constantly—making them automatic.

Here are ideas I use:

- Better than zero
- I can be sunshine wherever I stand
- Only the disciplined ones are free in life (said Eliud Kipchoge)
- There's nothing to teach.

I use "there's nothing to teach" as a reminder to move on after someone says something rude. That person will not learn from me. I move on.

I also use "there's nothing to teach" to move on when some thoughts about a past incident arise. In this way, I do not fall into a spiral of negative thoughts.

My interview with David Barron, a clinical hypnotherapist, focuses on empowering thoughts and patterns.

Interview with David Barron
(lightly edited)

Tom: David, recently we have been talking about what you call "using sublime emotions." Also, you talked about a part of your mission. Let's begin with a focus on your mission.

David: I have these words in my Manual under "How to treat your clients—and everyone else." I think of it as a subcategory of my Mission Statement.

Here is the material:

Every interaction, telephone call, text message, email, greeting, intake, hypnosis session, and follow-up session should fulfill one or more of these objectives for the client:

- *Provide reassurance*
- *Create anticipation*
- *Strengthen ego*
- *Reaffirm self-worth, self-esteem, positive self-image*
- *Validate their success*
- *Build optimism*
- *Reframe "failures" as valuable lessons*

If every interaction you have fulfils at least one of these objectives, you go beyond being just a good hypnotist, you become a good person. The world needs more people like you.

Tom: Excellent. Let's move on to sublime emotion.

David: I start with the Shadow as mentioned by Carl Jung. The Shadow is that part of us that we know is there, but we never want it to become public. It's the part of us that wants to strangle someone while we're smiling at them. It has the violent thoughts that we do not act on.

I noticed that when I nurture the Shadow that I get down feelings about humanity.

But then, by serendipity, I saw a singer in a video clip of *America's Got Talent*. The singer was Jane Marczewski. She went by the name Nightbirde.

The video on YouTube is dated 2021. She came out and talked in the most casual way that she had not been able to sing professionally for years because she was dealing with cancer. She had cancer in her liver, lungs, and spine.

She then sang a song she wrote called, "It's Okay." It was so authentic and so sincere. The judges cried. I cried.

Tom: I did, too!

David: I would watch it again and again just to get that feeling. I noticed that after watching the video again and again over five days—

Tom: Oh, wow.

David: That part of me—the Shadow—wasn't there...

Tom: So, this was an experience of sublime emotion for you?

David: Yes. Sublime meaning "to elevate." For example, dry ice doesn't turn to water and then into gas. It sublimates. It goes directly to gas. It sublimates. This experience with the video changed me significantly for several weeks.

Tom: Tell me more about "sublime emotion."

David: We're talking about having an experience that gives you an experience of "awe." It overwhelms your senses without turning it back inward to yourself. It radiates outward.

Other sublime emotions are a sense of connection, love, and gratitude.

I define sublime emotion as any feeling that turns you away from yourself, away from your ego.

Tom: If someone wants to nurture sublime emotion, what

do you suggest?

David: First of all, if you do any sort of devotional practice, thinking of a Higher Power, that's a way of connecting with sublime emotion.

Another way is understanding the dynamic between the ego and the Shadow. They are both there to protect you, but they don't necessarily make you feel good.

Another way is seeking connection. This is trying to look outside of yourself.

The last way is bizarre for most people. Ponder death. The Buddhists have this practice of meditating in a cemetery.

Tom: That's a stretch.

David: Yeah. A quote I came across is: "A dying person never needs a mindfulness course." And the final thing is practicing gratitude. Looking at the things around you. The fact that *you can take in a full breath of air and feel every part of it and enjoy it.* Anything you can be grateful for—for a moment. Your thoughts about yourself stop for a moment.

David Barron has served as a full-time hypnotist since 1998. He has devoted over 20,000 hypnosis hours, helping clients. He is the author of several books on hypnosis and persuasion. David says, "Hypnosis is a very personal journey. All you need is a willingness to change and to allow your hypnotist to guide you. Hypnosis isn't magical, even though the results can seem like magic. You will remember everything that happens and feeling amazing—when we are done." David is currently operating two hypnosis centers,

NewHampshireHypnosis.com

And EasternOregonHypnosis.com

In pondering what David Barron shared with us, I pull up

a parallel thought.

I say, **"Expression is the celebration."** Many people are waiting to impress someone or get some recognition. My thought is that *we enjoy "the doing."*

When is the right timing for transformation?

I interviewed Richard Bowling, the Founder of the MicroPod Engineer Entrepreneur Accelerator program. He provides insights about transformation.

Interview with Richard Bowling

Tom: You're the Founder of MicroPod which is the world's only transformational entrepreneurship program that helps engineers become entrepreneurs.

Richard: Yes.

Tom: What does transformation mean in this context?

Richard: Transformation is a loaded word that I have to explain. Transformation means that you're operating from different perspectives than you have now. Everyone has a set of beliefs, thoughts, and insights.

With my clients, I help them take their foot off the brake. The brake is their limiting beliefs. I help them keep their foot on the accelerator most of the time.

Tom: Excellent. You've mentioned to me something that is startling. You said, 'It's natural for people to second-guess their biggest dreams in life.' Starting from there, I'm curious.

How do you get the engineers to reward themselves so that they can consistently move forward?

Richard: There is an exercise that I give my clients. It's called MicroWins. It's a practice at the end of the day. They notice the two or three things that went well in their business endeavors for the day. Either in a journal or making a mental note. It's practicing the art of MicroWins. It is really powerful. You teach your brain to continue moving in a forward direction. Also, at the beginning of coaching sessions, we generally start with the things that went well from the previous week. Before we dive into the problems or challenges. **That sets up the brain. Hey, we're on the right track. We're mostly winning.** We're losing some of the battles. We're having troubles. But this is all related to the art of practicing MicroWins.

Tom: That's fantastic. It correlates to the research. The human brain is focused on the negative because that has survival value. **So, we have to train our brains to focus on the positive. We won't even remember what is good unless we track it.**

Richard, you've mentioned that *there is no power in having a great idea—the power is in the execution.*

Richard: Yes. I had a multi-million-dollar idea for over 20 years. The idea was for the world's first portable table tennis ball shooting machine. This sat, literally, in my closet for about 20 years. It didn't move forward until I actually got someone to help me figure out how to take this and turn it into a marketable product.

When you have a great idea, you need some system to bring it to life. It can be a mentor or coaching program. A lot of people have great ideas, but they don't know what to do with them.

Tom: And that's how you help your clients.

Richard: Yes. And transformation is a valuable element. When you have a series of shifted perspectives, you're operating on a transformed level. This causes changes in the way you see the world, how you operate, and how you act.

Richard Bowling, whose life passion is table tennis, is a former electrical engineer of multinational corporations; a former product engineer and product manager of a global sports company; a product inventor of a successful consumer product that generated over 8-figures in revenue and sold in numerous countries for over a decade. He is a 20-year researcher of coaching, personal development, peak performance, and practical neuroscience-based mindset tools.

Richard is currently a performance expert and mentor for engineer founders of mission-driven startups. His signature training program is the MicroPod Engineer Entrepreneur Accelerator program.

Richard has helped dozens of engineers to successfully and rapidly transition into entrepreneurship in numerous business verticals: AI, AR, blockchain, media, sustainable energy, sporting goods, real estate, personal development, and more…as SaaS/tech founders, engineering consultants, physical product inventors, investors, coaches, etc.

Richard's special offer: A complementary 45-minute entrepreneur strategy session. This complimentary entrepreneur strategy session is a $500 value. And it's made available ONLY for full-time, entrepreneurial, mid-career engineers (With at least three years of professional experience).

In this session, we will clearly identify your 3 biggest challenges in pursuing entrepreneurship, clarify your biggest goals, and see if the MicroPod accelerator program is the best vehicle to get you there.

Simply book here a 45-minute complementary entrepreneur strategy session

https://calendly.com/amarneo/45-min-entrepreneur-strategy-session-on-zoom-v

* * * * * * *

Gamify Grid #14 (Example)	
Action	Identify a limiting belief. Seek out a new belief you want to instill into your thinking patterns. Watch appropriate videos and read books (or blogs, etc.)
Token	Place a coin in a jar.
Date Start	2/7/20__
Date Completion	On-going
Self-Reward	Each week, watch a favorite TV show or YouTube video.

Now, it's your turn to fill in the Gamify Grid.

Gamify Grid	
Action	
Token	
Date Start	
Date Completion	
Self-Reward	

Important Point to Remember:
A transformation is shifting from limiting beliefs.

Power Questions:
What limiting beliefs do you hold? What other beliefs would help you more forward?

Chapter 16

Use the W.E.A.L.T.H System Timing and Planning (Part 2)

(Planning)

"You have three hours to film at San Luis Obispo Airport," Dewitt Ladd Rucker, the California Motion Picture Commissioner said.

It was my first feature film. I would film the big finish with characters running after an American Eagle airplane on the runway. (This was before the Sept. 11th Attacks in the United States.)

My intuition told me, "Something is going to go wrong."

So, I did important planning. I drew up storyboards of the essential images (shots) that I had to film at the airport with the plane.

I knew that, if it were necessary, I could get close-ups of the two characters running later. I would simulate the background later. Somewhere.

Good thing I planned. Because after *1 hour* of filming

with the airplane and 12 background actors—and the lead actors....

An airport official walked up to me and said, "Go. You must leave this runway."

Instead of arguing, I kept filming. I said to the co-producer, "Have the crew slowly move the lights. Have the background actors slowly leave the runway area."

All the while, I kept filming.

Until it was only the camera operator and myself (I portrayed one lead character.)

This was a triumph of planning for disaster—and saving the final scene of my feature film.

In fact, I later filmed some shots at the San Jose Mineta International Airport to finish the big climactic scene of the feature film.

I have learned to use the P.L.A.N. system:

P – prepare "tactics versus strategy"
L – learn
A – allow specifics with a possible failure
N – note Risk-Levels

1. Prepare "tactics versus strategy."

If you wanted more customers and you went to a website expert, this expert would have a vested interest in selling you the idea to massively alter your website. **Altering your website is a tactic.** We need to go deeper into the realm of strategy. It's possible that that process would require you to *go deeper into knowing the burning frustration of the customer that only you and what you offer can solve.*

Maybe you don't need a better website. Perhaps, you need ways of reaching out and filtering to the best potential customers who have a burning frustration.

A possible, better tactic would be to cold call this exclusive list of potential customers with such a burning frustration and pain.

In one case reported by Keith J. Cunningham, a website consultant recommended a $300,000 complete reimagining of her brand and website to a business owner. However, the business owner consulted her circle of other business owners. The discussion yielded a new strategy. Then, the real solution only cost $35,000. A big savings and a real solution.

Here's another vivid example as a metaphor of strategy versus tactic.

I visited my mother and father. My father said he wanted to move a heavy bookcase filled with delicate, fragile objects.

"Why are we doing this?" I asked him.

"That fan on top of the bookcase is rubbing against the curtains of the window," he replied.

"Wait a minute," I said. "The goal is to avoid having the fan interfered with by the curtains." I proposed a completely *different tactic.* We could take a small tube and have it hold back the curtains—away from the moving fan.

That's an example of going for a strategy and not just jumping in when someone just offers you the first tactic that bounces in their head.

When you make a powerful plan that will help you excel in increasing your wealth and well-being, be sure to prepare "tactics versus strategy."

"Sustained success requires strategy. And strategy requires:

- *Clarity on the obstacle or problem;*
- *A plan to overcome the obstacle;*
- *A structure for the allocation of resources;*
- *Prioritization of time and activities; and*
- *An analysis of risk."*

– Keith J. Cunningham

2. Learn

A risk can be worth taking if you're going to learn something crucial.

Here are three valuable questions.

- Will I learn something as I do this process?
- Will I form new alliances?
- Will I expand my capabilities and understanding?

Here's a bonus 4th question:

Can I make myself more valuable to the marketplace by learning something important with this process?

Carefully consider these questions and your answers. What can you learn here? This process can help you avoid making a big mistake that can cause big trouble.

3. Allow specifics with a possible failure.

A plan is not a plan if you don't have specifics that specify important standards of appropriate actions. By this I mean, if you have a plan to gain more customers, it's important to have a list of the potential people to contact.

You need to set a schedule for contacting these people each week. If you do not contact that number of people each week, then you can fail.

A plan with no possibility of failure is simply a "story."

Sometimes I share with my students and clients, don't tell your parents (or someone similar) your plan. Why? Because if you fail in some way, they'll say something derogatory including "I knew you couldn't do that. I knew that you'd fail at it."

You have to have someone trustworthy and who has an understanding of business and reality—to be your accountability partner.

At times, I consider some people I know as "civilians." They are *not* veterans of the journey of being an entrepreneur. They don't know what they're talking about.

Some of them tear things down that they don't understand. Fortunately, in my inner circle, I have people who coach me. These people support me. They want to see me succeed so they tell me the truth. They also help me find better ways to accomplish my real goals.

My important point is you need to have specifics:

- How many potential leads
- How many people to contact each week
- What you're going to do to contact them each week
- If that doesn't work what you're going to do next

All these specifics could lead to a possible failure. That means you are stretching and growing. This is a real plan. Something without specifics is merely a story. Many times, it's merely a fantasy story. You need a real plan.

If no possibility of failure exists, the plan does not have true specifics.

4. Note Risk-Levels

Every true plan includes risks. One foundational risk is the opportunity cost. It's the loss of potential gain from other alternatives. If you say *yes* to one thing, you're saying *no* to something else.

Here's an example.

When I was in college, I was the lead singer, keyboardist, and song composer for a band. I managed to create a situation to gain an investor to put in $20,000 for the band to create a music album. I received a $1000 advance fee, and my friend received a $1000 advance fee, too.

However, somebody connected to the money was going to run the whole show. I could tell that we would work so hard, but the music was going to turn out awful.

So, I gave back the $1000. But I had to cover the other $1000 that my friend had already used to buy music equipment. I was an independent student, meaning I had left my parents' home when I was 17 years old. (I did that to attend the college of my choice.)

I worked in the college mailroom and the science library. I had little cash, but I covered my friend's $1000 to end the project.

My intuition was clear that the risk of making garbage-music and wasting time was not worth it.

What I did was open and free up my future.

The next big thing I did was to write, produce, and direct a feature film. That experience then led to my career as an educator for college and graduate students.

Along the way, I met the love of my life.

Every decision led to something. I had to assess the risks all along the way.

We all need to be very careful about our risk levels.

Here are three vital questions:

- What is the number for the possibility of a crash?
- What is the number of a recovery?
- Is the loss unbearable?

I'll begin with the last question, Is the loss unbearable?

In an article in *the New York Times* by William Grimes, some vital details of what went wrong that led to the Challenger Space Shuttle disaster were noted:

During the afternoon and evening before the launch [of the Challenger Space Shuttle], Thiokol engineers, relying on data provided by Mr. Ebeling and his colleagues, argued passionately for a postponement of the launch in conference calls with NASA managers at the Kennedy Space Center in Florida and the Marshall Space Flight Center in Huntsville, Ala. They were overruled not only by NASA, but also by their own managers.

It was too dangerous for the Challenger Space Shuttle to be launched. History shows that the loss was unbearable—7 people.

Let's go back to the first question. What is the number for the possibility of a crash? What I mean by this is: "On a scale of 1 to 5, how likely is this going to end in a crash of big terrible trouble?"

I like to use a scale of 1 to 5. Why? It is easier intuitively to figure out the possible meaning. One might ask: "It's a 3. Why is it not a 2? Is there something we could do to lower the risk of a crash down to 2?"

On to the second question: What is the number of the recovery? How likely can you recover if this thing goes completely off the rails? For example, it may be possible to start a whole new division in your company without risking all the income or the equity in your company. It's worth looking into. A thorough plan would take into account all of the things we've talked about so far.

* * * * * *

When making an effective plan, you do better when you are careful with your choices.

Here is the *Choice Checker.*

We focus on 3 Questions:

1) Does this solve the problem or symptom?
2) How does this improve my life (my business)?
3) Do I prevent a bad consequence on the level of a peanut or coconut?

It's easier to remember this as S.I.P. (Solve, Improve, Prevent a Consequence). Think of *taking a S.I.P. of coffee to wake up.*

Let's go deeper…

1) Does this solve the problem or symptom?

We must guard against running enthusiastically in the wrong direction. That's a waste of time, money, and other resources. When you ask this question, you think on a deeper level. What is the true problem?

Let's say you do not have enough customers. Is this about your website or is this about your offer? Perhaps, **the real problem** is that your product does not solve a burning, red-hot pain point for your customer.

Altering your website is playing with a "symptom." It's not solving the real problem.

2) How does this improve my life (my business)?

You will pay for your choice. Is it worth it? Are you clear about the benefits? Are they essential to your life or business?

3) Do I prevent a bad consequence on the level of a peanut or coconut?

All choices have consequences. Often, you change something or do something for the first time. You get a benefit—but you may get unintended consequences.

Years ago, when I worked in a bank, I had the chance to move to another department. The pay was good. But I realized that was a "peanut" (or small concern). The bigger concern was the department had hypercritical people in it. I realized that this was a coconut.

A peanut is light to carry. However, a coconut can hit your head and do real damage. The coconut of working with hypercritical people stuck out to me. I did not want to live that way. It was a good decision to avoid that department. I soon moved on to being an educator. A much better fit for me.

* * * * * * *

Use the Daily Power Work Log

My nightmare had three leaders at my new job corner me. Often, when I'm sleeping, I face a situation in which I must give a speech on-the-fly to save a situation.

In this nightmare, I had to save my new job.

My impromptu speech yielded this Daily Power Work Log. First, we'll look at the form:

Daily Power Work Log	
Day: Monday (Day 1 of 39)	Date:
Concrete Objectives	(Example: Improved morale leads to improved productivity … More conversations for more sales)
Achievements	
Leaps forward	
Obstacles and Steps Taken to Overcome the Obstacles	
Growth Areas: Accomplishments so far	
Growth Areas: New Accomplishments	
Ask Leadership: "About what I've shared, what are you most interested in?"	
Ask: "What is most important to you?	
Ask: What adjustments would you like me to make?	
Daily Quota #1 (example: 10 phone calls to leads)	Actual Accomplishment (Example: 7 phone calls)
Daily Quota #2	Actual Accomplishment
Daily Quota #3	Actual Accomplishment

Brief Insights about the Daily Power Work Log

Some of my clients have worked for terrible bosses. To survive and even thrive in a hostile work environment, it is valuable to use a Daily Power Work Log. Often, one is called to justify one's actions and how much time it took to accomplish some tasks.

Additionally, I have worked with software engineers who faced getting stuck because someone did not give them something crucial.

Keeping a Daily Power Work Log helps one answer terrible questions. One of my mentors taught me: "The person with the best notes wins." I have worked in management positions in different industries. By keeping a work log, I have successfully defended myself from harsh questions. My clients have also found using the work log to be valuable.

I learned that if you have effective questions to throw back, as someone who is interrogating you, you come across as confident and competent. This reasoning is the starting part of having effective questions for leadership.

Asking for adjustments that the manager would like you to make helps you rise.

Confident people who are competent speak from evidence. You use your Daily Power Work Log to build the evidence that you are doing effective actions. You are meeting concrete objectives.

Additionally, entrepreneurs can use the Daily Power Work Log as a self-leadership tool.

* * * * * * *

A side note: I came up with the Daily Power Work Log

because the day before I coached a client. I guided him to focus on a work log for his new job.

By the way, for decades my personal mission continues as: "I help people experience enthusiasm, love, and wisdom to fulfill Big Dreams."

Gamify Grid #15 (Example)	
Action	Contact 6 excellent prospective buyers per day
Token	Place a jellybean in a jar.
Date Start	3/3/20__
Date Completion	On-going
Self-Reward	Take a brief walk after you complete your phone calls.

Now, it's your turn to fill out the Gamify Grid.

Gamify Grid	
Action	
Token	
Date Start	
Date Completion	
Self-Reward	

Important Point to Remember:
A plan with no possibility of failure is simply a "story."

Power Question:
How will you make your plan have specifics so there is a possibility of failure—and real success?

Chapter 17

Use the W.E.A.L.T.H System Habits, Help and Reserve (Part 1)

Renew your reserve—before a crisis.

Many of us experience multiple crisis events. It's important to have a reserve of personal energy. You will need that energy so you can perform at your best in such a crisis.

When I was 15 years old, I faced a crisis.

My father lifted me by the hair on my head. He had done this several times before. However, at 15, I had muscles and some martial arts training. I decided to end the chain of violence that included my paternal grandfather and my father. My paternal grandfather had died in a bar fight.

But striking my non-active Marine father would be stupid. It could lead to both of us in the hospital or worse.

The good news was I had a *reserve of calm*. How? Over a couple of years prior, I attended karate class. We were required to meditate for 2 minutes at the beginning and end of each class.

So, when my father lifted me by my hair and spit in my face yet again, I went calm inside.

I made a cool decision to punch a hole in the wall. My father* never lifted me by my hair nor spit in my face again.

That is the power of having a reserve.

A crisis may come up for you. Do what is necessary to have a reserve of energy and calm.

To this day, I have a daily habit of going quiet inside. Even if I only have 2 minutes to meditate, I do that each day.

What habit can you put in place, so you go quiet inside?

Why is this habit crucial? You will be tested. Angry co-workers, customers, friends, and family members will yell and more. When you can go instantly quiet inside, you will avoid making things worse. You won't yell or say things you can never take back. You will prevent yourself from doing something in anger that could cause you to be fired from a job.

* My father is a complicated person. He has done many good things for me. For example, he paid for those karate lessons. So, he gave me the gift of meditation. Over the years, we have had several good moments.

Gamify Your Wealth
Principle #10
Renew your reserve—before a crisis.

* * * * * *

By the way, here is the whole W.E.A.L.T.H. system…

The W.E.A.L.T.H. System:

W – work your confidence
E – elevate your influence
A – advantage
L – listen
T – timing
H – habits, help, and reserve

In my 20s, I was a film stuntman. One stunt I could not do was "submarining." This is when the stuntperson jumps a jet ski, dives, and zooms underwater. Then the person reemerges and races the jet ski away.

So, another stuntman did that stunt. But I was playing a lead part in the film. We needed a closeup of me on the jet ski.

The jet ski stuntman said, "I'll just aim the jet ski engine toward you and the backwash will make the illusion that you're racing along with the water swirling around you."

As the director and stuntman—in my 20s—I said, "Let's do it."

The film camera rolled. The jet ski stuntman aimed the jet ski backend and its engine at me. The water swirled. No—it punched. The powerful stream of water hit me solidly in the chest. The surge of the stream knocked me back 17 feet.

Once I was underwater, I stayed there. The surge continued over my head. I raised my hand. Waving. I was *not* going to rise out of the water and get hit in the face...by the powerful stream.

Eventually, the jet ski stuntman turned off his jet ski engine.

I learned an important lesson—

Do not compound a bad idea with a second bad idea.

Getting hit in the chest. Bad idea.

Rising quickly and getting hit in the face. **Worse idea**.

To audiences, I say, "If you don't have a reserve now, how can you handle more?"

When you have a reserve, you can make better decisions.

"Build a superreserve in every area: have more than enough."
– Thomas Leonard

Have more than enough. That takes us back to a definition of wealth: Having an abundance of a certain resource.

To make things better, it is crucial that you take action. You need a reserve to do that.

For example, To give good speeches, here's my action: *I rehearse.* Anytime I feel uneasy about an upcoming speech, I rehearse for a few minutes.

* * * * * *

To have a reserve, you need extra sleep, nutrition, and time away from work.

To have a reserve, you need extra energy and calm.

Life is tough, and it surprises you.

Your reserve helps you face fear.

It takes energy to face fear. Fear and anxiety can drain energy. Pain also drains energy.

The tough part about life is that nearly every day we have moments of pain. That's why it is crucial to have a reserve of energy.

In addition to energy, you also need a reserve of calm so that you can make excellent decisions that preserve your physical and mental health.

When you have a reserve, you can take a proactive approach to handling fear.

At one point I went into a big new situation, and it brought up huge fear in me. I prepared to write my first three novels in a genre I was unfamiliar with called urban fantasy.

I hired an editor to help me do an excellent job of serving the readers. This editor betrayed me. This person allowed terrible errors in the manuscript that would make the author look stupid. Such errors would create a terrible experience for the readers.

I was distraught that I had used up hundreds of dollars. I only had garbage to show for it. I didn't know what to do.

However, I was fortunate to have a reserve of energy and calm to think of a better idea.

This terrible editor lacking ethics betrayed me. I needed someone who was a true supporter of me and my writing. Who is that someone? Myself. How could I go beyond the limitations of one person's perception and still retain absolute devotion to doing good work?

I created a system I call ***5 for 5***.

I had a circle of 15 people. People who cared about me. People who I had helped with their projects. What if we could help each other every day?

Here's the structure of my *5 for 5 system*.

- They read their material to me for 5 minutes.
- I provide support and responses to their material.
- For five minutes, I read my material to the other person.
- They provide me with support and responses to my material.

To complete three novels in the *Jenalee Storm Series,* I talked with six people a day. That means I read 30 minutes of my material a day.

This was how I dealt with my fear of failing to do work that was valuable and that served the readers.

After developing such good material, I still needed to have a system for proofreading. Getting additional help for the proofing was necessary.

In my experience I just shared, you have a glimpse of my System for Handling Fear. It's called ***Face It—Flip It—Forward It.***

1. Face it.

When you're dealing with fear, if you don't name the fear, it has too much power in the shadows.

I had two sets of fear:

- If I found another stranger—a different editor—would they waste my money and also fail to support me to do excellent work?
- I was afraid of failing to do valuable work that serves readers.

I had to face these fears. Then I could come up with my *5 for 5 System.*

2. Flip it.

How can I turn the situation around if I can't trust a stranger to help me do good work?

How can I get help from people who love me, support me, and believe in me and my work?'

Once again, that's how I came up with my *5 for 5* system.

I flipped it. Afraid of a stranger who does not care?—*Flip It*—Go to people who already care about me.

3. Forward it.

"Replace worry with action." – Steve Chandler

Using my *5 for 5 system,* I was able to move my three novels forward. The people in my group were strong enough to tell me the truth. They alerted me to what could help me do an excellent job.

This was moving the project forward.

How can you approach something that you fear and use the system of Face It—Flip It—Forward It?

A sidenote: *My Face It—Flip It—Forward It System* is an important part of my science Code Access Reset™.

An Insight About Courage and Fear

Here is a classic quote:

"Courage is not the absence of fear, but rather the assessment that something else is more important than fear."
– Franklin D. Roosevelt

What can be more important than fear? Love. Hope. Trustworthiness. Happiness.

"3 Rules for Happiness: Something to do, someone to love, and something to hope for." – Immanuel Kant

"People talk about values. I value a pizza. What means more is to 'Aspire to Virtue.'" – Tom Marcoux

Aspire to what virtues? Love, Courage, Kindness, Loyalty, Persistence, Trustworthiness, Discipline.

"Most people want to avoid pain, and discipline is usually painful." – John C. Maxwell

"We must all suffer from one of two pains: the pain of discipline or the pain of regret. The difference is discipline weighs ounces while regret weighs tons." – Jim Rohn

Sometimes, a courageous action is to let go of old friends—especially false friends.

"No person is your friend who demands your silence or denies your right to grow." – Alice Walker

A final quote for this Chapter:

"We are happy when we are growing."
– William Butler Yeats

Gamify Grid #16 (Example)	
Action	Pick an action that requires you to demonstrate courage. Perhaps, it is giving a speech. Choose to rehearse for 10 minutes every day for three weeks.
Token	Place a coin in a jar.
Date Start	9/1/20__
Date Completion	9/21/20__
Self-Reward	Buy a film you love—on some form of media.

Now it's your turn to fill the Gamify Grid.

Gamify Grid	
Action	
Token	
Date Start	
Date Completion	
Self-Reward	

Important Point to Remember:
Having a reserve empowers you to act with courage.

Power Question:

What will you do this week to enhance your reserve of energy and personal calm?

A side note: Courage and Coachable are vital.

I say, ***Coachable is crucial.***

One year, I worked as a manager at a retail store. It was 8:47 pm one night. I was counting money at a cash register. It was a rough part of town.

A tall man stepped up to me and said, "Amigo, I'm a retired [police] officer. You're counting money in front of that window. No good."

"True," I replied.

From that day forward, I brought the money drawer to a second register that was deeper in the store. That's where I counted the money. This strategy avoided a crime of opportunity.

I was coachable.

What do you need coaching on?*

***Go to GetTheBigYES.com/courses for online courses from…**

Chapter 18

Use the W.E.A.L.T.H System Habits, Help and Reserve (Part 2)

Use the *Grow Wealth Habits Matrix*

It is reported that MC Hammer's net worth went from over $70 million during his heyday to a fall, landing at a loss of $13 million. He filed for bankruptcy in 1996. Some reports communicate that he had friends who caused him great difficulties.

On Bloomberg.com, it is reported that "Bill Hwang Had $20 Billion, Then Lost It All in Two Days."

This lines up with the classic comment: *It's not what you make, it's what you keep."*

On the other hand, reports say that Warren Buffet saved half of his income and kept investing—in his early years. At 14, Buffet purchased land and rented it out at a profit. His wife supported a modest lifestyle so they could continue to save a significant amount of income.

Another classic comment: *Be tremendously careful who you marry. This path flows to success or disaster.*

Some standup comedians say, "In a couple, you wind up at the level of the more stupid person."

Why? Because the smarter person gives in to the other one to "keep the peace."

With these details in mind, I wrote up the Grow Wealth Habits Matrix.

The Grow Wealth Habits Matrix

Grow Wealth Habits Matrix
Solve Better
Sell More
Make More
Keep More

1. Solve Better

If you have a business, it is crucial to solve a customer's Burning, Red Hot Pain Point. What could that pain point be? Are they afraid of something? What's costing them money? Did something else cause some frustration? What might destroy their business?

Pause and think about whether the customer already knows their big problem and big pain point. It's easier to get customers to buy if they already know what their big pain point is. If you must educate them about what you do and what they truly need, you may have significant problems.

To grow wealth, you need an extraordinary, magnetic offer.

Let's look at a few examples...

- Lose 57 pounds before summer
- Double your income and triple your time off
- Get your teenager to listen to you

Pain points are implied in the above examples.

What pain point can you solve for your customer?

2. Sell More

It feels obvious that if you sell more of what you offer you will increase your income. Many business owners are obsessed with growing from a base. However, imagine keeping the customers you have ***and*** selling more to them. Better than that, you can also gain more customers.

To gain more customers and to sell more to the customers you have, return to solving the burning red hot pain point.

You use the burning red hot pain point as part of your hook.

I say about a prospective customer:

He's hooked.
He's looked.
He's booked.

Pay close attention to the pattern and words you use when selling. For example, I learned that it is better to say *Would you like that?* than to say *Do you want that?*

Why? At any point the person can say, Yes, I would like that. That's an easier question to answer. I've seen this.

On the other hand, numerous people have trouble with the question, *Do you want that?* Their thoughts swirl around with:

Do I want this? I really want this. Do I need this? Do I deserve this? Is it okay for me to want this? What does this say about me as a human being if I want this? If I want this and I get this, will my friends think I'm stupid? Can I justify this to my spouse? Will my spouse simply lose it, if I bring home another one of these things?

You can see how it's easier to answer the question, Would you like this?"

3. Make More

Selling more seems to be a great solution. How about if it costs too much to fulfill each order? What if your profit margin is too small? To make more, you need to adjust all the factors of production and delivery.

4. Keep More

We return to the classic idea: It doesn't matter how much you make; it matters how much you keep.

On this topic, I think about this experience:

The cars collided. The airbag punched my face. My dinner almost leapt out of my mouth.

I felt the world had exploded taking away my hearing and my sight. I felt no control. I had been in the front passenger seat.

In life, you have probably noticed that much of the time you have no control. You can influence situations—often.

What can you do about "no control"?

Keep your money. Wealthy people save their money.

Here's an example.

Some time ago, my sweetheart and I decided to do a

Staycation—that's when you stay home and avoid big expenditures on air travel and other countries. (I have enjoyed giving speeches in various countries including New Zealand and Thailand. Travel can be joyful.)

My sweetheart and I enjoyed no stress of airports and more—during our Staycation.

We kept our money. Good idea!—because two weeks later we needed big money for repairs on a vehicle. This was a bad surprise. But we had funds. We control how we keep money.

Are you preparing for surprise bills and events coming your way? Are you saving your money?

Truly wealthy people save money. Many of them develop good habits of saving when they have little income (like Warren Buffet)—at the beginning of their wealth-creating journey.

Here is a useful money-saving habit: Talk through your purchases with an accountability partner.

Here's another habit: Avoid buying something when you feel bad. (Replace such a buying habit with some positive action. Perhaps, you take a walk or listen to empowering or soothing music. Maybe you call a supportive friend or see a therapist.)

In the book, *Your Money Or Your Life,* the authors Vicki Robin and Joe Dominguez, tell a story about a young woman who committed suicide.

The deceased woman's best friend is invited by the bereaved parents to go into their daughter's room.

"Keep anything you want as a memento of our daughter," the parents say.

The best friend discovers the deceased young woman

owned 21 white sweaters in unopened packaging. The young woman, suffering during her short life, bought these sweaters to soothe her feelings.

Imagine: Someone asks you, "Do you have something like a white sweater in your life?" What do you buy to soothe your feelings?

It's important to realize that many of us are kicked around by our negative feelings. We need habits in place so that we are *not* victims of these negative feelings. You need to be proactive about this.

What habit can you put in place to protect yourself from spending too much on things that provide temporary solace when you feel bad?

Will you have a friend or family member help you avoid buying stuff when you're feeling bad?

You need empowering habits…

Grow Wealth Habits Matrix (Example)	
Solve Better	Solve customer's Burning, Red Hot Pain Point of fear when pitching to get an investor's investment
Sell More	Offer 3 Levels: Interactive Workshop, Online Course, One-to-One Executive Coaching
Make More	Raise the price on all three levels
Keep More	Talk purchases through with one's spouse

Now, it's your turn to fill in the *Grow Wealth Habits Matrix.*

Grow Wealth Habits Matrix	
Solve Better	Solve customer's Burning, Red Hot Pain Point of ________
Sell More	
Make More	
Keep More	

Handle this situation: *Ruminate Versus Resolve*

To stay on track and make significant progress with expanding your wealth, it's valuable to shift away from ruminating to the space of resolve.

The definition of rumination includes: "Rumination involves repetitive thinking or dwelling on negative feelings and distress and their causes and consequences. The repetitive, negative aspect of rumination can contribute to the development of depression or anxiety and can worsen existing conditions." (American Psychiatric Association)

The definition of resolve includes ***"decide firmly on a course of action. .... firm determination to do something." (Oxford Languages)***

What is a solution for rumination?
Ask good questions.
Choose questions that help you shift your focus.

Let's say you were too blunt in your recent conversation with a friend.

Ruminating sounds like: "Oh, God. I'm going to lose my friendship with Aurora. Stupid! I shouldn't have said that..."

Instead, good questions include...

- What can I do now to remind Aurora that I care about her?
- What coaching can I get to help me do better?

Let's remember that resolve is: "The firm determination to do something."

Be sure to get coaching. Think things through.

Often, it helps to talk with someone who is safely on your side (perhaps, an executive coach). Vent with someone safe. Then you can empty "your fuel tank" of your upset feelings.

Resolve to learn and get better. You can perform better in your next encounter.

Important Point to Remember:

Grow Wealth Habits include:

- Solve Better
- Sell More
- Make More
- Keep More

Power Question:

In which area do you need to build better habits? ...

- Solve Better
- Sell More
- Make More
- Keep More

Chapter 19

List of Gamify Principles

1. Set the score and meaning.
2. Keep track of the days in which you complete a task. Start with "1" and carry on through "103" and beyond. As the number gets higher, you feel better than simply checking off that the task is completed.
3. Set up a good Gamify Pattern and you are trustworthy to yourself. Then, you are trustworthy to others. They want you to succeed.
4. Set an easy, simple task to get started, gain momentum, and elevate your morale.
5. When you complete your actions and log them, be careful about your conversations. Carefully choose who you will talk to and share your new experiences. Why? Some people are energy-drainers. Instead, you need to stay strong. Guard your energy and resolve.
6. When creating a new habit that feels like a strain … create a positive "welcome." This means you add something to lessen the pain involved. For example,

many people find it helpful to listen to good music at the start of a writing session.

7. If the action is boring, say, "It's just work." You let go of expectations.
8. As you log each time you complete an important action, you build two things. You build evidence that you are putting in the work. You also build your confidence that you are getting better at your chosen task.
9. When your Gamify Pattern grows stale, change something. Prepare for backsliding.
10. Renew your reserve—before a crisis.

Chapter 20 - Bonus

3 Principles of Code Access Reset™

My science of Code Access Reset™ is based on my work with thousands of clients, students, audiences, and more for over two decades.

Here is a portion of the proven techniques that are part of this science.

We focus on this useful process so you A.R.E. strong…

A – align with The Power of 3
R – rehearse
E – encode a Personal Code

1. Align with The Power of 3

When you focus on three areas, you can devote significant attention, energy, resources, and focus to create real progress. If you spread your energy and focus over ten areas, you cause yourself trouble. Your morale plummets. You fail to get things done. You lose credibility. You can even lose money because you pay for something but fail to devote sufficient focus, energy, and productivity to it.

Use the Power of 3.

This also applies to creating growth in your own business. Here's an example:

Power of 3:

a. Refine our message to fulfill the customer's Burning, Red Hot Pain Point.
b. Filter our Leads—present to truly qualified prospective customers.
c. Have a weekly quota of actions to present to these qualified leads. Close sales.

After you master 3 Focal Points, you can shift to three others.

2. Rehearse

Rehearsal helps you be at your best in the clutch moment. In basketball, the clutch moment is when the player shoots and scores—or shoots and chokes.

Basketball players relentlessly train.

I say,

You don't drill;
You don't know.

We need to train—that is, rehearse.

As a feature film director, I know how to direct a person to their best performance in the clutch moment.

Any time an actor or a speaker is performing, it is the clutch moment.

My work often revolves around my process called *Directed-Rehearsal*™.

Life has a series of clutch moments. **Rehearse, prepare, do well—and enjoy the adventure of your life.**

3. **Encode a Personal Code**

Until you create a "personal code" you do not own new material. How do you know if you know? You test.

For example, if I was going to give a speech on confidence, I would test if I knew my code of "The 3 C's."

The 3 C's of Confidence

- Confidence is built on evidence.
- Coachable
- Constant Rehearsing

If I fail to memorize a "code," I'm not ready to give the speech.

How do you encode a personal code?

a. Bring the ideas down to 3 crucial ideas.
b. Pick a word (like N.O.W.) or "3 C's" … (or something similar)
c. Make your 3 ideas memorable.
d. Rehearse daily. (Perhaps, 9 minutes before you brush your teeth in the morning.)
e. Practice self-testing. Verify you have access to your new skills.

More About Code Access Reset™

The Central Ideas:

1. Confidence is built on evidence. Prepare and *you know* you have an advantage.
2. Knowledge is just noise if you cannot recall it

instantly.

3. You need instant access to your new skill in the clutch moment.
4. If you don't practice retrieval, you don't own the information.
5. Practice self-testing. Verify you have access to your new skills.

I now close this Chapter with a powerful quote:

"Never surrender dreams. It is never too late to be what you want to be in the first place." – J. Michael Straczynski

Chapter 21 - Bonus

Elevate Your Life Before Time Runs Out

Are you living the life you wanted?
Many of us have been tossed off a path that we preferred.
I invite you to take small steps and move forward.

Here are phrases I often share:

- Better than zero
- Confidence is built on evidence. Prepare and *you know* you have an advantage.
- Motion brings clarity.
- Measure by your heart, not others' approval.

I created Code Access Reset™—a science and system that empowers my clients and audiences. The above elements are a portion of Code Access Reset™. These elements contribute to a person's elevating their life.

Let's dive in.

1. **Better than zero**

What can you do today that can elevate your life? At one point, I was losing weight and muscle mass. I decided to do weight training. For a particular exercise, I only did 5 motions—per exercise session. And I still gained muscle mass. 5 motions were better than zero.

Here's another example. 10 sit-ups a day over one year equals 3,650 sit-ups. That's better than zero.

What can you do now that is "better than zero"?

2. **Confidence is built on evidence. Prepare, and *you know* that you have an advantage.**

If you need to prepare for a job interview or a meeting, rehearsal is crucial. When you rehearse, you become clearer on what to say and how to say it. Rehearse and keep a log of your rehearsal sessions. Why? Then you have concrete evidence that you are putting in the work to prepare. Prepare effectively and you can do well.

When working with clients, I coach them using *Directed-Rehearsal.* This is my unique process because as a feature film director (and Spoken Word Strategist), I help people discover their best words and perform at their best.

Once again, confidence is built on evidence.

How can you put in rehearsal sessions and improve your real confidence?

3. **Motion brings clarity.**

I have worked with clients who said, "I'll do that when I have clarity."

That can cause a real problem. It's called stuck.

If you wait for absolute clarity before taking action, time can run out!

The opportunity can pass you by.

Take some action. Try something. Discover what works and what does not work.

Many of us need to bring something to the marketplace and see what real customers experience. Then we can adjust as we go along.

Working with real customers is a form of "collaboration."

"Collaboration is the elevation." – Tom Marcoux

I say, "When you take action, you step up the mountain. Then you can see new peaks you could not view from in the valley. You have new choices and opportunities. That is valuable clarity."

What motion would help you achieve some clarity? What small step can you take forward?

4. Measure by your heart, not others' approval.

No one else has your vision, your desires, or your destiny.

If I waited for approval, I would have missed so many opportunities. I would have missed directing my first feature film. I would have shied away from writing books in my "Darkest Secrets" series. Some people advised me to not use "Darkest Secrets." However, I went with my heart. For example, my book and an online course titled *Darkest Secrets of Film Directing* sell every year. The book debuted in 2013. That's several years of sales. And that's several years of helping filmmakers avoid big mistakes and dreams lost.

I say, "Expression is the celebration." By this I mean: When you do something creative, you can celebrate your courage and your accomplishment. You learn by doing.

By the way, what if someone says, "Don't do it"? But you

move forward anyway. You follow your heart and succeed. What will they do? Likely, they'll just shrug and say, "Meh. Whatever."

Their approval did not mean much in this situation.

Instead … measure by your heart, not others' approval.

These phrases help my clients and me elevate our lives. Life can be an adventure. You can grow, explore, and rise. The clock is ticking.

Make the best of today. Step forward.

Many great moments to you.

Chapter 22 - Bonus

Gamification: A Tool That Can Help People Build a Better Tomorrow

Gamification can be used to rise out of the valley and up a mountain. At a higher level, you can see new choices.

Let's look at some elements of Gamification.

1. Gamification is powerful for learning and education.

I often say, *Knowledge is just noise unless you can recall it instantly.* This is one of the central ideas of my science Code Access Reset™.

How do you know if you know something?

You test it.

Before I gave a speech at a recent conference, I tested myself. How? I gave myself a quiz on the three central points of my speech. I formed my points into a personal "code" of "A.I.M."

I tested if I knew each element. For example: "A" stood for "Align the specific to the universal."

"Researcher Dr. Nick Yee proposed one way to model the elements of what motivates gamers:
Action (e.g., objectives)
Social (e.g., competition)
Mastery (e.g., scoring)
Achievement (e.g., awards)
Immersion (e.g., roleplaying)
Creativity (e.g., customization)" noted by Richard Blankman

In my own use of gamification with clients, I have seen them excel with the use of the above elements. I started using gamification as part of Code Access Reset™ with clients. The reason is: I needed a way for clients to reliably complete actions that they "said" they intended to do.

2. Gamification can apply to communication.

"Gamification in internal organization communication leverages the human tendency to enjoy games and competition to pull people out of their office routine and get their attention in ways standard channels like email or town halls often fail to do. ... By making business initiatives and internal communication campaigns more interactive and enjoyable, successful gamification efforts can improve employee engagement by nearly fifty percent, leading to higher productivity and lower turnover. It can also increase participation in initiatives, motivation toward company goals, and retention of information." – James Irwin

Let's put it in four words: "Make it a game."

Recently, I was working with a client. I asked, "How can we make it a game, so you consistently show up each day and write your book?"

A team leader can engage employees to make a game of

many initiatives.

It begins with a question: "How about we make a game of who comes up with a better way to do XY, so we save 1 hour a week? Let's also figure out a good reward."

3. **Gamification shifts past human tendencies for inertia and self-sabotage.**

"Games are the only force in the known universe that can get people to take actions against their self-interest, in a predictable way, without using force. ... Gamification is a process of using game thinking and game dynamics to engage audiences and solve problems." – Gabe Zichermann, founder of Gamification.co and author of Gamification by Design

Gabe Zichermann says, "against their self-interest." This might apply to several individuals' tendency to want to sit around—and, perhaps, actually play video games.

The point here is that people have a natural tendency to enjoy games. So, you can shift past a natural hesitancy to do anything resembling "a chore."

Gamification is a tool that can be used for good or bad. It takes skill and intention.

If the intention is the good of all involved, gamification can help people build a better tomorrow.

Final Thoughts and Your Next Steps Forward

Congratulations on your progress with using the material in this book.

As I have shared:

Knowledge is just noise unless you can access it instantly.

What ideas and techniques do you want instant access to?

For example, one of the most powerful techniques I shared in this book is the *10-Minute Timer Reset.* I use this every day. I do not hesitate to write and create intellectual property.

It does not matter if I'm tired (I'm writing this at 2:40 AM). I set the timer. 10 minutes flies by like it is 1.5 minutes.

I click the timer again. I get so much done this way.

In this book, I have shared portions of my science Code Access Reset™ (C.A.R.) I say, "C.A.R. is your vehicle to transformation."

My question for you is…

Why do you want to expand your wealth?

"Use money to gain control over your time." – Morgan Housel

The more of your time you control the more freedom and ease your experience.

I have a phrase "It's just stuff." I do not buy much to "look at." Another phrase I have is: "It just gathers dust."

As researchers note, we gain more happiness with experiences with loved ones. We can enjoy solo experiences, too.

Will you expand how you serve others?

"I never begrudge an artist who has found an audience."
– David Bowie

"We are happy when we are growing."
– William Butler Yeats

"True happiness comes not when we get rid of all of our problems, but when we change our relationship to them, when we see our problems as a potential source of awakening, opportunities to practice, and to learn."
– Richard Carlson

In a feature film I directed, I played a lead character who lands a jet ski in the flatbed of a truck going 50 miles an hour.

In the editing room, we saw how I almost fell out of that flatbed. My face revealed my terror.

I almost died.

I was in my 20s. It's a wonder how many of us survive our 20s. So, I was a feature film director and film stuntman.

I learned that day that plans can go wrong.

When you plan, be sure to analyze risks and protect yourself and your future.

In later chapters of my life, I took further risks. I became an educator and served more than 5,000 students.

As a film stuntman, I took physical risks.

Imagine that you took action for the **right risks** for your better life.

I remember certain semesters when I would get the jitters before the first class of college students or graduate students. I wondered: "Do I still have the magic to capture the young people's attention?"

Having jitters is not a reason to stop. It is a signal to rehearse.

That's why I work with clients with my unique Directed-Rehearsal™ process.

Rehearse well and perform well.

What is important to you?

How will you use this book to elevate your life?

"Work is love made visible." – Kahlil Gibran

"When you take action, you're focused, and fear is a quiet voice in the background." – Tom Marcoux

Do you imagine that returning to certain parts of this book will help you? It takes rehearsal and memorizing so you master new techniques.

We do not merely read. We implement. We drill our new skills. We change. We transform.

Now is *your* time to take action.*

** See the next page for Next Steps that will help you.*

Many great moments to you,
Tom

Tom Marcoux
Communication Sage and Spoken Word Strategist

P.S. You can build on what you read with the following empowering courses… See the facing page.

Make Sure You Take the Next Steps

Enroll In Our Online Courses Now at The Tom Marcoux Institute.

GetTheBigYES.com/courses

"A must-have for your confidence and handling difficult personalities. Tom Marcoux really cares. Good Course."
– Jonathan Colton

"I found this course to be extremely well put-together, the advice was spot-on and intuitive, the teacher was relatable and direct. An excellent resource!"
– Jennifer Averry

"You'll be really prepared for whatever comes up when you pitch! You will learn to 'Answer the Investor's Bad Question with Your Own Story.' You can convince the investor to fund you."
– Mike Lamothe

Uplift Your Life with Tom's Online Courses

Better than About the Author: How Tom Marcoux Can Help You

When you want to more forward and create powerful results that feel great, work with Tom. Tom Marcoux serves as the Communication Sage and Spoken Word Strategist. He guides clients in his work as an Executive Coach. Need help to take the grand stage in the world?—with a pitch, new brand, a business, a TED Talk, speeches, video marketing, a book, a novel, a screenplay? Imagine your impact with all these elements optimized for *Your Leap Upwards to Success and Fulfillment.* Tom Marcoux has built his expertise with his life journey. Tom won a special award at the EMMY AWARDS, and his feature film went to Cannes Film market. He taught MBA students at STANFORD UNIVERSITY. *The San Francisco Examiner* has designated Tom Marcoux as "The Personal Branding Instructor." Tom taught effective Pitch delivery to Stanford Entrepreneurs and Silicon Valley Entrepreneurs ... and more.

Special Offer for Readers: Get Access to the Exclusive Video Series "Triple Your Persuasion Power to Close Sales" when you go to

GetTheBigYES.com/triple_persuasion_power

Methods You Can Trust

Tom Marcoux has coached thousands of CEOs, small business owners, startup founders, MBA students (Stanford University and other universities) and audience members.

Author of over 50 books, Tom has two required textbooks that served MBA students at Sofia University (on Authentic Marketing and Authentic Leadership Communication … the leadership book is *Shape the Future, Lead Like a Pro*). As a CEO, Tom has led teams in the U.K., India, and USA simultaneously.

Take the Grand Stage in the World

Tom helps with your Speech – Pitch – Video Marketing – Networking … and rehearsing for your critical life-changing meetings. **Contact Tom at GetTheBigYES.com**

International Speaker Tom Marcoux has energized audiences from New York to New Zealand (plus Silicon Valley, California, Thailand, and more).

Tom's Methods Empower Clients to Get Their Best Results

- ⇨ "I'm truly grateful to Tom Marcoux for essential tips that helped me win the Grand Prize of the Pitch Competition—the Igniter Summit in Bangkok, Thailand." – Neeraj Aggarwala, CEO/Founder of Sportido
- ⇨ "Tom Marcoux has coached me to make my speeches compelling and powerful. He has helped me prepare for the media. Do your career a big favor and engage Tom Marcoux, the Spoken Word Strategist." – Dr. JoAnn Dahlkoetter, author of *Your Performing Edge* and Coach to CEOs and Olympic Gold Medalists
- ⇨ "Tom Marcoux coached me to get more done in 10 days than other coaches in 2 years." – Brad Carlson, CEO of MindStrong, LLC

Your Next Steps

#1. See **vital online courses** available through the Tom Marcoux Institute at GetTheBigYES.com/courses

- Success Secrets: Confidence and Skills to Handle Toxic People
- Ignite Your Sales Success
- Convince Investors to Fund You
- Darkest Secrets of Persuasion and Seduction Master: How to Protect Yourself and Turn the Power to Good

#2. See free Special Videos at GettheBigYES.com/nextstep

#3. Apply for a **Free Hidden Breakthrough Strategy Session** at GetTheBigYES.com/nextstep

#4. Hear Podcasts on iTunes ***Succeed Even If*** (over 60 podcast episodes on topics including enhance confidence, speak with no fear, and more)

#5. Look inside Tom's 50+ books at a major online retailer https://amzn.to/2Iq5WQl

#6. *Subscribe* to YouTube Channel ***Succeed Even If*** at https://bit.ly/2W9LaIf

Even More *Best Results*

"Tom Marcoux coached me so well that when I faced a high-level prospective client, it was amazing. It was unbelievable how easy it felt to me. I wasn't nervous because Tom guided me through all the rehearsing. Tom emphasizes *'Words – Strategy – Rehearsal.'* I was more-than-ready because we had worked through all the possible scenarios. Tom also empowers me with his expertise with building a unique and compelling brand: logos, language, media releases, speech-writing, videos and more." – Tim Cox, the Business Systems Strategist

"Tom helped me unearth deeply emotional and humorous moments in my speech to move the hearts of the audience." – Krishna Noru

"Tom Marcoux has been an NAB Conference favorite [speaker] for six years. And he is very energetic." – John Marino, Vice President, National Association of Broadcasters, Washington, D.C.

One of Tom's books rose to #1 on Hot New Releases in Business Life (and in Business Communication)—at a major online retailer.

"Tom Marcoux helped me in ways no other coaches could. Anyone who has the opportunity to work with Tom is blessed for sure." – Junie Moon Schreiber

"Using just one of Tom Marcoux's methods, I got more done in 2 weeks than in 6 months." – Jaclyn Freitas, M.A.

(In a few pages, see an excerpt from Tom Marcoux's book, *Darkest Secrets of Persuasion and Seduction Masters: How to Protect Yourself and Turn the Power to Good.*)

Partial List of References

1. *100 Ways to Motivate Yourself, 3rd Edition* by Steve Chandler
2. *$100M Offers: How to Make Offers So Good People Feel Stupid Saying No* by Alex Hormozi
3. *Atomic Habits: An Easy & Proven Way to Build Good Habits & Break Bad Ones* by James Clear
4. *The Checklist Manifesto: How to Get Things Right* by Atul Gawande
5. *The Confidence Code: The Science and Art of Self-Assurance—What Women Should Know* by Katty Kay and Claire Shipman
6. *Connect* by Tom Marcoux
7. *Convince Investors to Fund You* by Tom Marcoux
8. *Decoding Greatness: How the Best in the World Reverse Engineer Success* by Ron Friedman
9. *Dopamine Nation: Finding Balance in the Age of Indulgence* by Dr. Anna Lembke
10. *For the Win, Revised and Updated Edition: The Power of Gamification and Game Thinking in Business, Education, Government, and Social Impact* by Kevin Werbach and Dan Hunter
11. *Game Thinking: Innovate Smarter & Drive Deep Engagement with Design Techniques from Hit Games* by Amy Jo Kim
12. *Louder Than Words: Take Your Career from Average to Exceptional with the Hidden Power of Nonverbal Intelligence* by Joe Navarro with Toni Sciarra Poynter

13. *Pitch Anything* by Oren Klaff
14. *The Power of Habit: Why We Do What We Do in Life and Business* by Charles Duhigg
15. *The Psychology of Money* by Morgan Housel
16. *Relax, You Don't Have to Sell: How to Make Sales Without Being Pushy* by Tom Marcoux
17. *The Road Less Stupid* by Keith J. Cunningham
18. *Soar: Nothing Can Stop You This Year* by Tom Marcoux
19. *Time Management Secrets the Rich Won't Tell You* by Tom Marcoux
20. *Wealth Habits* by Candy Valentino
21. *The Worst Is Over: What to Say When Every Moment Counts* by Judith Acosta, LCSW and Judith Simon Prager PhD
22. *The Writer's Solution: Crush Your Self-Doubt* by Tom Marcoux

* * * * * *

Bonus Chapter

Entertainment, Gamification and Communication Power

What do we remember?
Something short.
Researchers also note that what rhymes sounds true.
When I talk about gamification I say,

Gamify
Or fail to fly.

I have also added comics to how I communicate elements

of my science Code Access Reset™ and how it includes elements of gamification.

I created something I call *Twisted City*. These are comic images that communicate ideas with an entertainment twist.

My work continues to transform.

I remember these ideas:

"Creativity is allowing yourself to make mistakes. Art is knowing which ones to keep."

- Scott Adams, creator of the comics, Dilbert

On the Next Page, I introduce the primary characters of *Twisted City*.

To add a game element, we can ask, "Which of these 4 characters would say "____"?

(See the next page.)

Preliminary sketches by Tom Marcoux

(See an Excerpt from one of Tom's 50+ books on the next page.)

Excerpt from

Darkest Secrets of Persuasion and Seduction Masters: How to Protect Yourself and Turn the Power to Good

by Tom Marcoux, Communication Sage and Spoken Word Strategist—Executive Coach

. . . for 27 years I have been taking action to protect people.

And now is the time for me to protect you with the Countermeasures I reveal in this book.

Every human being needs to be able to break the trance that a Manipulator creates. You need to make good decisions, so you are safe, and you keep growing—and you are not cut down and crippled.

This Darkest Secrets material is so intense that I first released it only with the counterbalance of my most energizing and uplifting books, *Soar! Nothing Can Stop You This Year* and *Year of Awesome: How You Can Use 12 Success Principles including 10 Seconds to Wealth.*

An interviewer asked me: "Who can be the Manipulator?"

A co-worker, a boss, a salesperson, someone you're dating, and someone you think is a friend.

Now is the time—this very minute—for me to write this book to protect you.

I must speak the truth.

These Darkest Secrets of "persuasion masters" are ...

Wait a minute! Let's say it plainly: These are the Darkest Secrets of masters of manipulation. Throughout this book, I will call these people what they are: Manipulators.

Dictionary.com defines "manipulate" as "To influence or manage shrewdly or deviously.... To tamper with or falsify for personal gain."

In this book, we will look on a manipulator as one who deviously influences someone with no concern about that person's well-being, and who causes harm to that person.

Here is the first Darkest Secret:

Darkest Secret #1:
Manipulators Make You Hurt
and Then Offer the Salve.

Manipulators would invite you to go out in the sun for hours and then sell you the salve to soothe your burns. The problem is that we don't notice that this is what they're doing.

For example, you're considering the purchase of a house. A Manipulator asks the question, "So, where would you put your TV?" This question is designed to put you into a trance.

Dictionary.com defines "trance" as "a half-conscious state, seemingly between sleeping and waking, in which ability to function voluntarily may be suspended." Let's condense this: In a trance, you may not be able to function freely.

Here is the second Secret:

Darkest Secret #2:
Manipulators Put You into a Trance.

To protect yourself, you must learn to use Countermeasures to Break the Trance.

All the Countermeasures (actions you can take to break the trance) in this book will make you stronger and more capable of protecting yourself.

Now, we'll view the third Secret:

Darkest Secret #3:
Manipulators Care Nothing for You and Human Decency: They'll lie, cheat, and do whatever they need to do so they win—but their charm masks all this.

Let's return to the example of a Manipulator selling you a house. A Manipulator does not pause for an instant to see if you can truly afford the new house. The Manipulator would neglect to mention that you will not only have your mortgage payment of $1200. There will be additional costs: home repairs, property tax, water, electricity, homeowner's insurance, and more. The Manipulator only emphasizes what he or she knows you want to hear: "Look! $1200 is better than the $3000 you're paying for rent, which is just going down the toilet. And the $1200 is an investment."

Let's go back to **Darkest Secret #1:**

Manipulators make you hurt and then offer the salve.

The Manipulator has you feeling good about the solution (salve) and feeling bad about your current life situation.

How? A Manipulator will make you hurt through questions such as:

- What bothers you about paying $3000 a month for rent? (The Manipulator will use a derisive tone when he says the word *rent*.)
- What is *not* smart about paying rent on someone

else's house instead of investing in your own house?
- How do you feel about your children walking in the neighborhood where you live now?

Do you see how these questions are designed to make you hurt enough so that you'll buy?

An interviewer asked me, "Tom, aren't these good arguments for purchasing a house?"

"What we're looking at is the *intention* of the influencer," I replied. "Let's look at our definition of a manipulator as one who deviously influences someone with no concern about that person's well-being, and who causes harm to that person. If the person truly cannot afford the house, he or she will be harmed by buying it. If the manipulator conceals the truth, the manipulator is doing harm. That's the important difference."

Some friends of mine are ethical and helpful real estate agents who truthfully reveal the whole situation and help the purchaser achieve her own goals.

In this book, we are talking about another type of person; that is, unethical Manipulators.

* * *

In any given moment, we need to remember the tactics Manipulators use. We will focus on the word D.A.R.K. so you can remember details easily and protect yourself from Manipulators.

D — Dangle something for nothing

A — Alert to scarcity

R — Reveal the Desperate Hot Button

K — Keep on pushing buttons

1. Dangle Something for Nothing

What do conmen and conwomen do to seize your

attention? They make you think you're getting a "steal."

I recently saw a documentary in which a conman on a street in England showed a toy that looked like it was dancing. This fake product was actually dancing because of a hidden, invisible thread. The conman was dangling something for nothing. The Entranced Buyer thought he was getting something worth $20 for only $5. That was the trick. The Entranced Buyer felt that he was getting $15 extra of value for his $5. What the Buyer really got was something worth nothing. Similarly, I know someone who purchased a copy of a Disney movie from a street vendor in San Francisco. She brought the copy home and it was unwatchable—and the street vendor was never seen again.

An old phrase goes, "A conman cannot con someone who is *not* looking for something for nothing."

How to Protect Yourself from "Dangle Something for Nothing"

Stop! Get on your cell phone and talk through the "deal" with someone you know who thinks clearly. Go home. Think about it. Do some research on the Internet. Listen to your gut feelings. If the salesperson or conman is too insistent, get away from that Manipulator. Get quiet. Have a cup of water. Cool down. Break the Trance!

Break the Trance and Identify the Crucial Detail

Earlier, I mentioned that a Manipulator puts you into a trance. An added problem is that we put ourselves into a trance. For example, as you read this, are you thinking about your right toe? Most likely not (unless you stubbed your toe recently). The point is that we only focus on a tiny percentage of what is going on in our life.

Several years ago, I caused myself trouble because I put

myself into a trance. I discovered that under certain conditions, friendship can make you nearly deaf. Here's how: I was producing a song for a motion picture. A good friend was singing backup in the chorus. Because of our friendship, I wanted him to sound great. I completely missed the Crucial Detail. In this kind of situation, the Crucial Detail is that what truly counts is how the lead singer sounds! I made a song that I could not release. What a waste of time and money! I had put myself into a trance.

In any situation in which the Manipulator is "dangling something for nothing," we often fall into a trance and miss the Crucial Detail. The most important detail is not that we're saving money if we order before midnight tonight. What counts is whether the product creates a lasting, crucial benefit in our lives. And is the benefit of the product worth the cost? Some people even program themselves to make mistakes by saying, "I can't pass up a bargain." The bargain is not the Crucial Detail.

Secrets to Break the Trance

This is the process of B.R.E.A.K.S. It will help you remember the proven methods to break a trance.

B — Breathe

R — Relax

E — Envision

A — Act on aromas

K — Keep moving

S — Smile

Secret #1: Breathe

Remember *Secret #1: Manipulators make you hurt and then offer the salve.* The Manipulator wants to put you into a state of being that fills you with a sense of urgency and anxiety.

Oh, no! I'm going to miss the sale! Stop this highly vulnerable state. Take a deep breath.

End of Excerpt from ***Darkest Secrets of Persuasion and Seduction Masters: How to Protect Yourself and Turn the Power to Good***

Purchase your copy of this book (paperback, eBook—or Audiobook) at a major online retailer's website.

See Free Chapters of Tom Marcoux's over 50 books at http://amzn.to/ZiCTRj

Tom has 23 audiobooks at a major online retailer's website.

Many great moments to you.

www.ingramcontent.com/pod-product-compliance
Lightning Source LLC
LaVergne TN
LVHW050632100826
845148LV00011B/1847

* 9 7 8 0 9 6 2 4 6 6 0 8 3 *